D0713880

Richard Nixon

James Madison

THE JAMES MADISON LIBRARY
IN AMERICAN POLITICS

Sean Wilentz, General Editor

The James Madison Library in American Politics of the Princeton University Press is devoted to reviving important American political writings of the recent and distant past. American politics has produced an abundance of important works—proclaiming ideas, describing candidates, explaining the inner workings of government, and analyzing political campaigns. This literature includes partisan and philosophical manifestos, pamphlets of practical political theory, muckraking exposés, autobiographies, on-the-scene reportage, and more. The James Madison Library issues fresh editions of both classic and now-neglected titles that helped shape the American political landscape. Up-to-date commentaries in each volume by leading scholars, journalists, and political figures make the books accessible to modern readers.

The Conscience of a Conservative by Barry M. Goldwater

The New Industrial State by John Kenneth Galbraith

Liberty and the News by Walter Lippmann

The Politics of Hope and The Bitter Heritage: American Liberalism in the 1960s by Arthur M. Schlesinger, Jr.

Richard Nixon: Speeches, Writings, Documents, edited and introduced by Rick Perlstein

Richard Nixon

Speeches, Writings, Documents

Edited and introduced by **Rick Perlstein**

PRINCETON UNIVERSITY PRESS
PRINCETON AND OXFORD

Published by Princeton University Press,
41 William Street, Princeton, New Jersey 08540
In the United Kingdom: Princeton University Press,
6 Oxford Street, Woodstock, Oxfordshire OX20 1TW

Library of Congress Cataloging-in-Publication Data

Nixon, Richard M. (Richard Milhous), 1913–1994.
[Selections. 2008]
Richard Nixon : speeches, writings, documents /edited
and introduced by Rick Perlstein.
p. cm. — (The James Madison Library in American politics)
Includes bibliographical references and index.
ISBN 978-0-691-13699-8 (pbk. : alk. paper)
1. Nixon, Richard M. (Richard Milhous), 1913–1994—Archives.
2. Presidents—United States—Archives. 3. United States—Politics
and government—1945–1989—Sources. 4. Speeches, addresses,
etc., American. I. Perlstein, Rick, 1969– II. Title.
E838.5.N52 2008
973.924092—dc22 2008014928

British Library Cataloging-in-Publication Data is available

This book has been composed in Sabon with Helvetica Neue
and Didot display

Printed on acid-free paper. ∞
press.princeton.edu
Printed in the United States of America

10 9 8 7 6 5 4 3 2 1

Contents

General Editor's Introduction ix
Introduction xiii
Bibliographic Note lxxi

I. Youth

1. From *RN: The Memoirs of Richard Nixon* (1978) 3
2. Two letters (1923 and 1924) 5
3. "Our Privileges under the Constitution" (1929) 7
4. From the Frank Gannon interviews (1983) 14

II. Congress

5. "The Hiss Case—A Lesson for the American People" (January 26, 1950) 19
6. The "Pink Sheet" (1950) 60
7. The "Checkers Speech" (September 23, 1952) 64

III. Vice President

8. "When you go out to shoot rats" (March 13, 1954) 83
9. The "Kitchen Debate" (July 24, 1959) 88

10. Opening Statement, The Great Debate: Kennedy v. Nixon (September 26, 1960) 97

IV. Comeback

11. "Gentlemen, this is my last press conference" (November 6, 1962) 105
12. "The irresponsible tactics of some of the extreme civil rights leaders" (February 12, 1964) 113
13. "Appraisal from Manila" (November 4, 1966) 117
14. "What Has Happened to America?" (*Reader's Digest*, October 1967) 121
15. "Asia after Viet Nam" (*Foreign Affairs*, October 1967) 128
16. "The first civil right of every American is to be free from domestic violence" (August 8, 1968) 145

V. President

17. "To lower our voices would be a simple thing" (January 20, 1969) 153
18. "The present welfare system has to be judged a colossal failure" (August 8, 1969) 163
19. "The great silent majority of my fellow Americans" (November 3, 1969) 170

20. "The postwar period in international relations has ended" (February 18, 1970) 191
21. Four Vietnam Statements (1970) 200
22. Two political statements (1970) 209
23. "Our best days lie ahead" (August 15, 1971) 217
24. "One China" (February 24, 1972) 223
25. "He can undisappear if we want him to" (June 23, 1972) 232
26. "Her name was Tanya" (August 23, 1972) 238
27. "There can be no whitewash at the White House" (April 30, 1973) 242
28. "I am not a crook" (November 17, 1973) 255
29. "I made clear there was to be no coverup" (April 29, 1974) 259
30. "My mother was a saint" (August 9, 1974) 269

Index 277

General Editor's Introduction

The American political tradition is preeminently practical. Ideas, sometimes of genuine philosophical grandeur, have certainly motivated the getting and exercise of power. American political rhetoric, whether delivered in speeches, written in pamphlets and treatises, or incorporated in state papers, has inspired countless millions, at home and abroad. But the heart of the day-to-day American political system involves less elevated yet essential tasks, including overawing or even betraying a political opponent, cajoling and compromising in order to win legislation (or, sometimes, to defeat legislation), or building a winning coalition out of disparate political constituencies. Ironically, two of the most profound, and profoundly American, documents in American history, the United States Constitution and the Federalist Papers, offered and defended, with great intellectual care, a national polity that insures the primacy of the practical, rejecting the flight toward abstraction and uncertainty in favor of a realization that men are not angels, and that governments must be designed with a pragmatic sense of the danger of human frailty as well as the promise of human achievement.

Richard Milhous Nixon, a man of numerous frailties, was in many ways an odd and even unique figure, but his career describes an important arc in the practical politics of modern America. Born to humble circumstances, he rose through careers in law and politics with a combination of iron will and sharply honed resentments. For more than two decades prior to his election to the White House in 1968, Nixon shrewdly navigated the shoals of Republican Party politics, shifting from conservative anti-Communist crusader to moderately pro–New Deal Eisenhower "modern Republican," until, after suffering heartbreaking defeats in 1960 and 1962, he emerged as virtually a party unto himself, with pragmatic ties to Republicans across a wide political and ideological spectrum.

Liberals thought of him as acceptable enough compared to the Republicans' hard-right Goldwater wing; the hard Right, although always suspicious of him, fell into line in response to the entreaties of former Dixiecrat Strom Thurmond of South Carolina, guaranteeing Nixon the nomination and then a narrow victory in the presidential election of 1968. Thereafter, Nixon continued to tack, sometimes with the wind, sometimes against it, a political genius in his own mind, never letting the s.o.b.'s of his inner dramas get him down, always plotting revenge and, when necessary, comeback—even after the Watergate scandal and related revelations offered persuasive evidence that, as president, he had systematically violated his oath of office to preserve, protect, and defend the

Constitution. By dint of human folly, hubris, and sheer good luck, the Constitution fended off attacks by the eminently practical men of Nixon's Oval Office who had confused Nixon's own political supremacy with the nation's well-being.

Rick Perlstein, who has written extensively and with great originality on Nixon and his presidency, has here assembled a rich collection of documents that, in effect, form in Nixon's own words the autobiography he did not write—a volume more revealing in many ways than the several volumes of memoir and reflection that Nixon actually did write. Although nobody would call Nixon a preeminent political thinker, his thinking as well as his actions and rhetoric tell a great deal about the development of American politics during the decades after World War II. The denouement of his career in the White House, leading to the first and only departure of any president apart from those who died in office, will forever be one of the classic episodes in U.S. history—one with enduring lessons about the letter and the spirit of the Constitution that formed our imperfect but ameliorable Union.

This volume represents something of a departure from the earlier titles in the James Madison Library in American Politics, because it offers not a single discrete work but a collection of selected letters, speeches, and other documents from an important figure—in this case a politician and officeholder. It is less of a manifesto or a set of observations about American politics than the chronicle of a career that reached the highest levels of electoral politics and government. Similar volumes will appear in future, alongside other variations on the basic format—part of the library's mission to capture as many facets of the American political experience as possible.

Sean Wilentz

Introduction

Rick Perlstein

I

In the fall of 1967 Richard Nixon, reintroducing himself to the public for his second run for the presidency of the United States, published two magazine articles simultaneously. The first ran in the distinguished quarterly *Foreign Affairs*, the review of the Council of Foreign Relations. "Asia after Viet Nam" was sweeping, scholarly, and high-minded, couched in the chessboard abstractions of strategic studies. The intended audience, in whose language it spoke, was the nation's elite, and liberal-leaning, opinion-makers. It argued for the diplomatic "long view" toward the nation, China, that he had spoken of only in terms of red-baiting demagoguery in the past: "we simply cannot afford to leave China forever outside the family of nations," he wrote. This was the height of foreign policy sophistication, the kind of thing one heard in Ivy League faculty lounges and Brookings Institution seminars. For Nixon, the conclusion was the product of years of quiet travel, study, and reflection that his long stretch in the political wilderness, since losing the California governor's race in 1962, had liberated him to carry out. It bore no relation to the kind of rip-roaring, elite-baiting things he usually said about Communists on the stump in the eleven Republican elections in which he had previously participated.[1]

Nixon's second article that fall was published in the nation's most widely read monthly, *Reader's Digest*. The *Digest*, consumed by around twenty million Americans, was the opposite of *Foreign Affairs* in every way: jingoistic, sappy, and as likely as not to identify any given liberal-leaning opinion-maker as a self-serving bamboozler. Nixon's article was called "What Has Happened to America?" and its mood was demagogic, angry, and apocalyptic. Its subject was a summer of deadly race riots that had left "the United States blazing in an inferno of urban anarchy." His solution was a law-and-order crackdown. The riots, the article said, showed that American society had become "among the most lawless and violent in the history of the free peoples," a common sentiment among the conservatives of the day. The argument, however, added a signature Nixonian touch. When it came time to affix blame, he downplayed the role of the rioters. Instead, he blamed the same people who were the intended *audience* for "Asia after Viet Nam": liberal elites. "Our opinion-makers have gone too far in promoting the doctrine that when a law is broken, society, not the criminal, is to blame," he wrote. "Our teachers, preachers, and politicians have gone too far in advocating the idea that each

[1] "Asia after Viet Nam," *Foreign Affairs* 46, no. 1 (October 1967).

individual should determine what laws are good and what laws are bad."[2]

Two articles, two audiences, two different messages: that's politics. Richard Nixon, however, the twentieth century's quintessential political man, pushed the contradiction yet further. The *Foreign Affairs* essay concluded with a curious metaphor. "Dealing with Red China is something like trying to cope with the more explosive ghetto elements of our own country," he said. "In each case dialogues have to be opened; in each case aggression has to be restrained while education proceeds; and, not least, in neither case can we afford to let those now self-exiled from society to stay exiled forever. We have to proceed with both an urgency born of necessity and a patience born of realism, moving by calculated steps toward the final goal." Of course, "dialogue" and "education" were the liberal opinion-making elites' prescriptions for what to do about "the most explosive ghetto elements of our country"—not what conservative Republicans would call for. In the service of selling liberals his foreign policy vision, he was willing to ventriloquize their script.

The trope of the "two Nixons" has been a staple of commentary about the man since the 1950s. Pundits tended to understand the problem serially:

[2] "What Has Happened to America?" *Reader's Digest*, October 1967.

they would announce that they detected a newfound maturity in the demagogue they had called "Tricky Dick," now making sound, nuanced, and humane contributions to the public debate; then, like clockwork, he would start talking about "anarchy" and blame it all on the liberal elites. And the pundits would announce in rueful tones that the "old Nixon" had returned—and then the cycle ("Is there a 'new Nixon'?") would repeat itself a few years later. The pundits never got it quite right. Richard Nixon was driven by a consistent passion to make sound, nuanced, and humane contributions to public debate. And he also, and at the same time, inhabited a mental world, as his arch-foe Adlai Stevenson would put it, of "slander and scare," of "smash and grab and anything to win." This part of him was driven by an unstinting rage for control, a need to dominate and even humiliate opinion-making elites—whom he also saw as architects not merely of society's moral degradation, but of the political humiliation of Richard Nixon.[3]

A day in the life of Richard Nixon was never either/or when it came to this bifurcated orienta-

[3] Fawn Brodie, *Richard Nixon: The Shaping of His Character* (New York: Norton, 1981), 312, 327, 356–58. For Nixon's youth generally, see Renée K. Schulte, ed., *The Young Nixon: An Oral Inquiry* (Fullerton: California State University, Fullerton, Oral History Program, 1978).

tion; it was always both/and. He needed elites, and hated them; he hated elites, and wanted to be accepted among them. He could be open-minded and open-hearted, and he could rage for control. It had always been so, even before his political career began, and even until his political career was ended. To many Americans—who also simultaneously revered and resented elites—it was the soul of his political appeal.

II

Richard Milhous Nixon was born on a winter day in 1913 "in a house," as he put it sonorously in his 1978 memoirs, "my father built." The little plaster-frame cottage—you can still visit it at the Richard Nixon Library and Birthplace in Yorba Linda, California—was across from a new irrigation ditch that promised for the first time to make good on the Chamber of Commerce boast that this desert outpost was a good place to grow citrus. For the children of this cactus-covered town it made for a bit of fun: they could swim in it, or at least wade in it. All except the Nixon boys. When Frank Nixon saw his boys in the canal, he would grab them by the scruff of the neck, haul them out, push them in, taunt them, then throw them in a few more times. One of Richard Nixon's biographers, reflecting upon the image, speculated a kid "might well have felt that his father was trying to drown him like an unwanted puppy."[4]

For most farmers that ditch helped bring a decent crop. Not Frank Nixon, who was filled with the kind of self-destructive abstemiousness that is sometimes labeled pride. "I won't buy fertilizer until I raise enough lemons to pay for it," he said, though in Yorba Linda's "loaf-sugar" soil—it tended to clump—you couldn't grow lemons without fertilizer. Frank and his family went bust. California wasn't supposed to be like this.[5]

Frank Nixon was a tempestuous man who loved to argue, even to the point of driving much-needed custom from the grocery store and gas station he built in a former church. The store did well nonetheless, and for a time the family nestled comfortably within the 1920s middle class. Richard Nixon would ever vacillate between feelings of pride and feelings of shame toward his dirty-necked, lusty spitfire of a father, between apologizing for him and boasting about him, between desperately reaching for success to honor him and desperately reaching for success to repudiate him. Frank Nixon was also his son's mentor in his schoolboy debating career. Dick won often, though his high school coach bemoaned his "abil-

[4] Richard Nixon, *RN: The Memoirs of Richard Nixon* (New York: Grosset & Dunlap, 1978), 3; Brodie, *Richard Nixon*, 40.

[5] Leonard Lurie, *The Running of Richard Nixon* (New York: Coward, McGann, and Geoghegan, 1972), 29.

ity to kind of slide around an argument instead of meeting it head on."[6]

His mother, Hannah, Nixon famously put it in his farewell address after he resigned the presidency in disgrace, "was a saint." She was a soft-spoken and devout Quaker, but there was one subject upon which she didn't always tell the truth: her second son, Richard. The family's superstar, the one on whom the family hopes had been pinned, was the first son, Harold, who was graceful and loquacious, where Richard was an awkward loner. Harold came down with tuberculosis, and Hannah took him to recuperate in the hot, dry air of Prescott, Arizona. That required setting up a second household, during the Depression, which almost bankrupted the family. Then Nixon's youngest brother died in a freak accident for which Richard seemed to hold himself accountable. When Harold died, Hannah told an interviewer, Richard "sank into a deep, impenetrable silence. . . . From that time on it seemed that he was trying to be three sons in one, striving even harder than before to make up to his father and me for our loss."[7]

For her part, Hannah Nixon would come to recast Richard in her mind as an impregnable figure of destiny, a bringer of miracles. She would later

[6] Brodie, *Richard Nixon*, 40.
[7] Lurie, *Running of Richard Nixon*, 22.

tell interviewers that Richard had been born the day of an eclipse (he wasn't), and that his ragged and forlorn family had sold land upon which oil was found immediately afterward (they hadn't). This family was a churning stewpot of shame and stubborn pride, haunted by a sense of unearned persecutions, ever convinced they were better than what the world would let them be.[8]

As a schoolboy he hadn't a single close friend, preferring to cloister himself with a book up in the former church's bell tower, hating to ride the school bus because he thought the other children smelled bad. His brilliance and awesome application won him a scholarship to Harvard. But he could afford only to stay home and attend Whittier, a fine little Quaker college unknown anywhere else. There, Nixon came into his own socially, but in a peculiarly Nixonian fashion. One biographer described a cartoon of seniors in the Whittier yearbook "lounging informally, talking and laughing. . . . Nixon at the very center . . . but while the rest are clearly enjoying themselves, Richard stands alone, neatly dressed, completely devoid of emotion—solemnly dominating the group, but not part of it." That image provides a template for understanding his political career.[9]

Finding himself excluded from Whittier College's single social club, the Franklins, this most

[8] Brodie, *Richard Nixon*, 35.
[9] Lurie, *Running of Richard Nixon*, 27.

unfraternal of youth organized the remnant into a fraternity of his own. Franklins were well-rounded, graceful; they moved smoothly, talked slickly. Nixon's new club, the Orthogonians, was for the strivers, the commuter students, those not to the manor born. Forever more, Nixon would gather together those who believed themselves put upon by the sophisticates, setting himself up as both one of them and apart from them—their leader. For instance, he surprised those who spotted him as an up-and-comer by seeking out a berth on the House un-American Activities Committee (HUAC), a collection of poltroons widely seen to have permanently humiliated themselves with the Hollywood Ten circus; then he engineered his investiture as its most respected voice. His famous "Checkers" speech of 1952, fighting to preserve his place as General Dwight D. Eisenhower's vice presidential candidate against charges he had an improper campaign fund, rocketed him to a new plateau of popularity because of his success in speaking as an everyman put upon by an aloof and arrogant boss. He misquoted Lincoln: "God must have loved the common people—he made so many of them."[10]

[10] Chris Matthews, *Kennedy and Nixon: The Rivalry That Shaped Postwar America* (New York: Free Press, 1997), 24–25; Brodie, *Richard Nixon*, 113–15; Tom Wicker, *One of Us: Richard Nixon and the American Dream* (New York: Random House, 1991), 80–11; Brodie, *Richard Nixon*, 271–89.

Those who felt themselves condescended to by the sophisticates were everywhere in the majority. They formed an excellent constituency for a political career. In 1969, in one of his most famous speeches, he gave this abstraction a permanent name: the "Silent Majority."

III

America's liberals saw themselves as the tribunes of the common people, Republicans as enemies of the common people. *Liberals* had been the ones to write the New Deal social and labor legislation that let ordinary Americans win back a measure of economic security during the Depression. *Liberals* had led the war against fascism, World War II, a war conservatives opposed. They had been the architects of the postwar consumer economy that built the first mass middle class in world history. But by the 1950s history caught them in a bind: via the boom they helped build, ordinary laborers were comfortable enough to entertain appeals from Republicans styling themselves as tribunes of the common man. The "Checkers" in the Checkers speech referred to Nixon's absurd implication that his persecutors were demanding he return the "little cocker spaniel dog" a supporter had sent his little girls as a gift—a red herring to deflect attention from the very specific financial charges at hand. The idea that a maudlin appeal to sentiment could trump ordinary people's recognition of the "real" economic issues at hand drove his ideological adversaries around the bend.[11]

The ensuing debate over Richard M. Nixon would track the main contours of America's political divisions to this day. "The man who the people of the sovereign state of California believed was actually representing them" was actually "the pet and protegé of a special interest group of rich Southern Californians," one liberal paper editorialized of the Checkers speech. The pundit Walter Lippmann called it "the most demeaning experience my country has ever had to bear." The in-house humorist of Stevensonian liberalism, Mort Sahl, suggested a sequel. Nixon could read the Constitution aloud to his two daughters; Pat, his wife, could sit within camera view, gazing lovingly upon him while knitting an American flag.[12]

But liberals' hatred of him as a phony populist didn't start with Checkers. Under the tutelage of Murray Chotiner, a cutthroat California political operative whose legal specialty was defending bookies, Nixon learned a uniquely nasty cam-

[11] David Greenberg, *Nixon's Shadow: The History of an Image* (New York: Norton, 2004), chapter 2.

[12] Frank Mankiewicz, *Perfectly Clear: Nixon from Whittier to Watergate* (New York: Quadrangle Books, 1973), 63; Stanley Kutler, *The Wars of Watergate: The Last Crisis of Richard Nixon* (New York: Norton, 1992), 34; David Broder and Stephen Hess, *The Republican Establishment: The Present and Future of the GOP* (New York: Harper & Row, 1967), 152.

paign style that specialized in turning economic populists out of office with the message that they were actually feckless aristocrats, selling out America to her enemies. For his first campaign, in 1946, he framed his opponent, the well-bred Jerry Voorhis, as a handmaiden of Communists even though Voorhis had proposed a bill outlawing the American Communist Party. In 1950, running for Senate, he called his opponent Helen Gahagan Douglas (a sophisticate married to Hollywood leading man Melvyn Douglas) "pink right down to her underwear"—and sent out 500,000 fliers, printed on pink paper, tying her to "the notorious Communist party-line Congressman from New York" Vito Marcantonio. Upon his victory, the senator-elect attended a chic Georgetown party hosted by columnist Joseph Alsop. W. Averell Harriman, son of a railroad baron and a distinguished ambassador who had traveled to California that campaign season to help Helen Gahagan Douglas, was announced. He spied Nixon, and, turning on his heels, barked: "I will not break bread with that man!"[13]

Nixon had an explanation for the sophisticates' contempt, and it had nothing to do with his campaign style: they hated him for beating Alger Hiss.

[13] Wicker, *One of Us*, 33–45; Greg Mitchell, *Tricky Dick and the Pink Lady: Richard Nixon vs. Helen Gahagan Douglas—Sexual Politics and the Red Scare, 1950* (New York: Random House, 1990).

Hiss had been a legendarily distinguished public servant and protégé of some of the most distinguished men in the Washington Establishment. At a HUAC hearing in 1948, a disheveled and strange *Time* magazine staffer and Communist apostate named Whittaker Chambers accused Hiss of having been a secret Communist. Hiss demanded time before the committee to clear his name. Well-dressed, well-bred, and well-spoken, Hiss so convincingly voiced his claim that he hadn't known "Whittaker Chambers" that HUAC was prepared to drop the matter. Only Richard Nixon objected. Tipped off by freelance anti-Communist investigators, he had noticed a hole in his testimony: Hiss had never said he hadn't known Chambers. He had just said he hadn't known a man *named* Whittaker Chambers.[14]

Exhibiting the obsessive work ethic that marked his career, Nixon established a record that rendered the notion that the two had not known each other virtually impossible. And yet Hiss, nailed dead to rights, arrogantly stuck to his story. And maddeningly, his Establishment sponsors kept defending him—insinuating that *Chambers* was the villain. President Truman called the case a "red herring." Chambers, an apocalyptic man, thought he knew why: Communists in high places

[14] Sam Tanenhaus, *Whittaker Chambers: A Biography* (New York: Random House, 1997).

were pulling strings behind the scenes. Richard Nixon harbored the more prosaic theory a lifetime of resentments had prepared him for: the Establishment was protecting one of their own.

The case became a national soap opera, dragging on for years—a 1940s media equivalent of the O. J. Simpson trial, or the Monica Lewinsky scandal. In one unforgettable twist, Chambers produced clinching evidence—State Department documents on spools of microfilm—from a hollowed-out pumpkin on his farm. Finally, on January 25, 1950, like Al Capone being put away for tax evasion, Hiss was sentenced to five years in federal prison for perjury. The second-term Congressman found himself promoted, in a weak and leaderless Republican Party, as a debating partner of the Democratic president. And in a monumental special order House speech that effectively launched his Senate campaign, Nixon assimilated the Hiss case's "Lessons for the American People" to his favorite narrative: the swells putting one over on the plain people, loosing anarchy upon the land.

Forever more, Richard Nixon would remain convinced that the swells would never forgive him for finding them out. As he put it rather fantastically in the conclusion to his epic eighty-three-page account of the Hiss case in his 1962 book *Six Crises*: "For the next twelve years of my public service in Washington, I was to be subjected to an utterly unprincipled and vicious smear campaign. Bigamy, forgery, drunkenness, thievery, anti-Semitism, perjury, the whole gamut of misconduct in public office, ranging from unethical to downright criminal activities—all these were among the charges that were hurled against me, some publicly and others through whispering campaigns that were even more difficult to counteract."[15]

In fact he provided plenty more organic reasons for his critics to hate him. Running for vice president, he assailed Secretary of State Dean Acheson for his "color blindness, a form of pink eye toward the communist threat in United States"; Democratic nominee Adlai Stevenson for his "Ph.D. from Dean Acheson's College of Cowardly Communist Containment"; and Acheson, Stevenson, and President Truman for having become "traitors to the high principles in which many of the nation's Democrats believe." In 1954, in his biannual role as tireless itinerant campaigner for Republican congressional candidates, he said that the new Republican White House occupants had "found in the files a blueprint for socializing America" and claimed possession of "a secret memorandum of the Communist party" proving "it is determined to conduct its program within the Democratic Party."[16]

[15] Richard Nixon, *Six Crises* (New York: Doubleday, 1962), 82.

[16] Greenberg, *Nixon's Shadow*, 109, 120; Brodie, *Richard Nixon*, 313–15, 329.

In 1956, the Republican ticket again featured Nixon despite the Republican Establishment's revived attempt to get him dumped. President Eisenhower had recently suffered a heart attack, so Adlai Stevenson concentrated his second presidential campaign almost exclusively against the horror that Nixon would become president. "As a citizen more than a candidate," he said, "I recoil at the prospect of Mr. Nixon as a custodian of this nation's future, as guardian of the hydrogen bomb." And "Our nation stands at a fork in the political road. In one direction lies a land of slander and scare; the land of sly innuendo, the poison pen, the anonymous phone call and hustling, pushing, shoving; the land of smash and grab and anything to win. This is Nixonland. America is something different."[17]

Of course, however, insinuating that your opponent would nuke the planet was also slander and scare, and spared not the innuendo. Adlai Stevenson had coined a useful word: Nixonland. But it more accurately describes a two-sided engagement. The first group, Stevenson's, took it as axiomatic that if Richard Nixon's values triumphed, America was done for. The second, Nixon's, took it as axiomatic that if Adlai Stevenson's values triumphed, America was done for. Once

[17] Greenberg, *Nixon's Shadow*, 62; John Kenneth Galbraith, *A Life in Our Times: Memoirs* (Boston: Houghton Mifflin, 1981), 346.

again, as with Checkers, the confrontation helped determine the contours of the "red" versus "blue" political world we know now.

IV

That other Richard Nixon, the nuanced foreign policy guru, was not AWOL during these years. He came into maturity. The dominant pre–World War II foreign policy tradition on the Republican right was isolationism. Traces of isolationist distrust survived in conservatives' approach to the Cold War—especially in their opposition to alliances like the North Atlantic Treaty Organization and aid programs like the Marshall Plan. Richard Nixon, to the dismay of his conservative constituents, decisively broke with this tradition.

Some trace it to his experience as the only House freshman to travel to Europe with the congressional study committee that helped frame the Marshall Plan. But the boyhood *National Geographic* reader—"All through grade school my ambition was to become a railroad engineer," he wrote in his memoir—had always harbored a cosmopolitan streak. And his proselytization for internationalism was one of the things that made him so attractive to Dwight D. Eisenhower, who had made extinguishing Republican isolationism a major political goal. In 1953, Ike sent his new vice president to survey the hottest new Cold War flashpoint: Vietnam. Nixon returned to find his stature profoundly enhanced, especially among elite opinion-makers—an important pattern in his political career, these stature-enhancing foreign trips. The following spring he delivered a major address before the nation's newspaper editors on the complexities of arresting the spread of Communism in Asia. The same man who spoke of Dean Acheson's College of Cowardly Communist Containment, paradoxically, was well on his way to earning his Achesonian merit badge as a foreign policy sage.[18]

It came just in the nick of time. In 1955 Eisenhower had his heart attack. In 1956, given the even chance Nixon might end up president, Ike issued instructions for him to campaign as a statesman fit for the leadership of the Free World—to "give 'em heaven," instead of giving them hell. The injunction made Nixon supremely uncomfortable. When Eisenhower fell behind in the polls, and Nixon was finally given license to breathe fire, Nixon later reflected, "I felt as if a great weight had been lifted off me." Nothing more agonized Richard Nixon than to leave a humiliation unanswered.

Eisenhower pulled out a second term; the vice president enhanced his national stature yet more

[18] Wicker, *One of Us*, 51–55; Nixon, *RN*, 3; Brodie, *Richard Nixon*, 316.

with two remarkable performances overseas, first in South America, then in the Soviet Union. In Lima, Peru, his party was met by a hail of rocks from a crowd shouting, "Fuera Nixon! Fuera Nixon!" ["Down with Nixon!"], and, occasionally, "Meura Nixon! Meura!" ["Death to Nixon!"]. He got out of his car to shame his attackers, debating them face-to-face. In Caracas, Venezuela, his motorcade was intercepted by a mob attempt on his life. As in Peru, Nixon put his most admirable qualities on fullest display: a refusal to back down under intimidation, and a remarkable calmness in a crisis. As stones sprayed the supposedly shatterproof glass of his limousine, a Secret Service bodyguard reached for his revolver. Nixon decided the sound of gunfire would send the crowd into a frenzy that would make escape impossible. It was the kind of presence of mind for which battlefield commanders win medals. He was handsomely rewarded for his grace under pressure: wherever Nixon went he got standing ovations. For the first time, the Republicans' presidential nominee–apparent was starting to look, to the Establishment, like presidential timber.[19]

Another trip the next year cemented the judgment. Cold War tensions were at a point of relax-

[19] Nixon, *RN*, 177–78; Nixon, *Six Crises*, 183–234; Earl Mazo, *Richard Nixon: A Political and Personal Portrait* (New York: Harper & Brothers, 1959), 203–46.

ation. The United States was invited to exhibit at a trade fair in Moscow's Skolniki Park, and Nixon traveled to Russia to dedicate the American pavilion. During a ceremonial stroll with Premier Khrushchev, an extraordinary impromptu exchange took shape. Several nights later, what became known as the "Kitchen Debate" ran on TV. Basically, the dialogue consisted of Nixon preaching the glories of the consumer luxuries even the lowliest American steelworker could afford and arguing that economic competition was preferable to nuclear war; Khrushchev, in turn, would affect delight at the Cold War olive branch ("I have to say I cannot recognize my friend Mr. Nixon") and retort that Soviet steelworkers could afford equally nice homes. As a "debate," mediated through awkward translation, it hardly amounted to much (*Khrushchev*: "We have a saying: if you have bedbugs you have to catch one and pour boiling water into the ear." *Nixon*: "We have another saying. This is that the way to kill a fly is to make it drink whiskey"). But by catching up in sour-grapes contradictions the man American audiences had been taught to fear more than any other (first, Khrushchev bragged, "We have such things"; then he disparaged, "They are merely gadgets"), Nixon emerged looking more presidential than ever.[20]

[20] Brodie, *Richard Nixon*, 378–87.

And it was this identity as the seasoned statesman, not the attacker of cultural elites, that Nixon chose to carry into the fight of his life—his 1960 presidential campaign against the more inexperienced John F. Kennedy. Friends advised Nixon to sneak before the public imprecations of his opponent's unpopular religion, his mendacity on the issue of his health, his loose interpretation of his marriage vows. Instead, Nixon decided to campaign as a gentleman. He would recite the number of meetings he had taken with the president (173), the times he had sat with the National Security Council (217, presiding 26 times), the number of countries he had visited (54), the presidents and prime ministers with whom he had had "extended discussion" (44, plus an emperor and a shah)—adding always, "incidentally," "I have talked with Khrushchev." But once more, as in 1956, the plan proved an awkward fit.[21]

Television had played an outsized role in Nixon's rise. Now it would play an outsized role in his fall. The first presidential debate in the history of television was broadcast from Chicago on Monday, September 26. Nixon came in with a commanding lead in the polls. Posterity remembers his drawn appearance, the five o'clock shadow, his arrogant refusal of makeup, the bead of perspiration that lingered on his lower lip. An

[21] Ibid., 421.

even greater contribution to his loss might have been the predebate pep talk from his running mate, Henry Cabot Lodge, an Establishmentarian par excellence, who implored him: "Erase the assassin image." Kennedy opened the debate with a sort of dirty trick. The subject of this first of three debates was supposed to be domestic affairs, but Kennedy came out swinging with a scouring assessment of America's "struggle with Mr. Khrushchev for survival." Kennedy then smartly twisted his supposed liability—his inexperience—into an asset, assailing the Republicans as backward, sclerotic, and old, presiding over "the lowest rate of economic growth of any major industrialized society in the world." Nixon, a stickler for obsessive preparation, wasn't prepared for this.[22]

Under ordinary circumstances he might have reached into his voluminous Red Scare trick bag, perhaps repeating his smear on Adlai Stevenson's patriotism from 1956 when that Democrat had criticized the Republicans' economic record: he could have said Kennedy had "attacked with violent fury the economic system of the United States." Instead he acted like a deer in the headlights. He spent the rest of the evening agreeing with his adversary point by point. For instance, when Kennedy announced a bold new program to provide medical care for the aged. Nixon re-

[22] Ibid., 414.

sponded, “We are for programs, in addition, which will see that our medical care for the aged are—is—are much—is much better handled than at the present time”—the present time being that of his own incumbent administration. In the five weeks that followed, Nixon never recovered. The hair's-breadth loss in his quest to lead the Free World haunted him for the rest of his life. It certainly informed his campaign two years later for governor of California. Aiming at Sacramento, he highlighted his ability to handle Khrushchev. On election eve he made the gaffe of saying he was running for “governor of the United States.”[23]

A man who had come within an inch of leading the Free World running for a mere governorship: there was something pathetic in the exercise. Initially he had led the incumbent by sixteen points. Then he was challenged in the Republican primary by a far-right nonentity who still got about a third of the vote; then California's ascendent Far Right abandoned Nixon in the general election. (They hadn't trusted Nixon since he had gone on TV to disavow Joseph McCarthy on behalf of the administration in 1954.) The previous Republican governor endorsed the Democrat. Bumper stickers appeared around the state: “Would You Buy A Used Car From This Man?” California would not.

[23] Ibid., 459.

Nixon lost his second election in as many years. He was only forty-nine years old. On election night he was so dejected he was refusing to make a concession speech. Aides talked him into it. It turned out to be the most famous speech in his life—a rambling, barely coherent rant that concluded, famously, "You won't have Nixon to kick around any more, because, gentlemen, this is my last press conference." What was even more damaging to his reputation, if that was possible, was what he said next, off microphone, loud enough for *Time*'s reporter to quote: "I gave it to them right in the behind. It had to be said, goddammit. It had to be said."[24]

Judged *Time*: "Perhaps he had risen too far too fast. . . . Barring a miracle, his political career ended last week."

V

Nixon even seemed, for an interval, to take the notion to heart. He moved to New York and cashed in as a corporate lawyer, and made arrangements with a political writer to produce a

[24] Joseph Lewis, *What Makes Reagan Run? A Political Profile* (New York: McGraw-Hill, 1968), 64; Jules Witcover, *The Resurrection of Richard Nixon* (New York: G. P. Putnam's Sons, 1970), 13–23; "California: Career's End," *Time*, November 16, 1962, accessible at http://www.time.com/time/magazine/article/0,9171,829391-2,00.html.

book on the 1964 presidential election. It would have been his second book; in 1962 he published an impressively introspective memoir entitled *Six Crises*. He wrote it, he said in the preface, on the advice of President Kennedy, who had told him a politician should publish a book because "it tends to elevate him in popular esteem to the respected status of an 'intellectual.'"[25]

A new force was rising in the Republican firmament: Barry Goldwater, the Arizona senator drafted to run for president by an insurgent cabal of far-right activists. At first, Kennedy had welcomed the chance to face him. Then, in the spring of 1963, Kennedy embraced the most sweeping civil rights legislation in history. The anti-Kennedy backlash was furious—and gained surprising support in the industrial North. Experts who had been projecting a Kennedy landslide wondered now whether Goldwater, as a stalwart foe of the civil rights bill, might not be able to pick him off. In a poll of Republican leaders, only 3 percent said Nixon would make a good candidate. He was too liberal.[26]

Everything changed with Kennedy's assassination, including Richard Nixon's plans. A national wave of contrition followed the trauma: last

[25] Nixon, *Six Crises*, x.

[26] Rick Perlstein, *Before the Storm: Barry Goldwater and the Unmaking of the American Consensus* (New York: Hill & Wang, 2001), 204–15.

month's political common sense now seemed a flirtation with something ugly and un-American. A horror at all things labeled "extremist" swept the land. Goldwater's political currency deflated overnight. And for Nixon, the years spent cultivating an image as a middle-of-the-road statesman finally paid political dividends: in Gallup's first postassassination poll, Nixon was Republicans' first choice.[27]

He spent the first half of 1964 on a kabuki campaign to get himself drafted by acclimation, bidding for Barry Goldwater's supporters. He started spouting right-wing clichés like "Planning an economy eventually ends in planning men's lives," and turned his back on his reputation as a pro–civil rights Republican by delivering a ferocious attack in Cincinnati against black parents who protested school segregation in the urban North by keeping their children out of school for a one-day strike. He followed it with a spring trip to Vietnam, proclaiming upon his return, "There is no substitute for victory." Goldwater's book on foreign policy was called *Why Not Victory?*[28]

He refused to believe the party insiders who told him that the Goldwater insurgents had the nomination wrapped up. He hired operatives to set up clandestine campaigns to engineer "sponta-

[27] Ibid., 253.

[28] Ibid., 253, 261–62, 288–89, 298, 310–11, 317–18.

neous" primary upsets, and squandered his necessary reputation as a conciliator between Republican factions when his fingerprints were discovered on a "stop Goldwater" movement in California. He groveled before Goldwater, reassuring him of his undying respect. Then, at a governors' conference prior to the Republican convention, he announced that if Goldwater's conservative views weren't repudiated, a "tragedy" would befall the Republican Party. At a breakfast of Republican governors he opened the floor for questions in the hopes he would be implored to save the party. Reporters learned that the silence that followed lasted a full fifteen seconds.[29]

At that, he pivoted 180 degrees ideologically for the second time in months. He warmly introduced Goldwater at the convention (though he set up a secret command center just in case he could drum up a last-minute draft). And while every other Republican of national stature chose either to sit out Goldwater's presidential campaign or to work behind the scenes for Lyndon Johnson, Nixon gave 156 speeches for the doomed ticket in 36 states. Once again the Establishment wrote his obituary, this time in bafflement at his bizarre attempts at conciliation with the conservative faction that had just led the Republican Party over a cliff. "Each of his carefully calculated moves in 1964 was fol-

[29] Ibid., 331–32, 353, 358.

lowed only by his own further political destruction," columnists Rowland Evans and Robert Novak concluded.[30]

Nixon got the last laugh. He understood what the pundits did not: that the delegates he addressed at the Republican National Convention would be more or less the same group that would choose the 1968 nominee. And that the conservatives had taken over the party from the ground up, and weren't going away just because Barry Goldwater won only six states. According to party rules, the states that had gone for Goldwater were rewarded with extra delegates, which meant that Southern states would control the nomination in 1968. Quietly but energetically, after Goldwater's defeat, Nixon began lining up Southern support with assurances a President Nixon would not enforce federal civil rights laws. His most crucial and loyal recruit was South Carolina's segregationist senator Strom Thurmond. It was the beginning of Nixon's infamous "Southern Strategy."[31]

The defining issue in the election—the reason Republicans did so well—was the anti–civil rights backlash. The summer was marked by shocking race riots and debate over a failed bill to outlaw racial discrimination in the sale and rental of hous-

[30] Ibid., 388, 390–92; Rowland Evans and Robert Novak, "The Unmaking of a President," *Esquire*, November 1964.

[31] Rick Perlstein, *Nixonland: The Rise of a President and the Fracturing of America* (New York: Scribner, 2008), 87–89.

ing. Richard Nixon, campaigning for no fewer than sixty-six Republican congressional candidates, hardly said a word on these issues. He focused on Vietnam. It was an issue, in 1966, whose partisan salience was limited: both parties hosted nearly equal complements of hawks and doves. Nixon's own positions were confusing, shifting from week to week: we should escalate; we should negotiate; we should bomb more; we should pause the bombing; we should pour in troops; pouring in troops would be a scandal; military defeat would bring on World War III. What he was up to was evident only in retrospect.

Nixon retainer Leonard Garment disarmingly revealed in his 1997 memoir what Nixon already then believed about Vietnam: that the war could not be won. Politically, the realization seemed to free him to say just about anything. And what he said at any given moment bore the following pattern: it was the opposite of what President Johnson was saying. The strategy seemed to be to force the president to address Nixon, previously beneath notice, in anger. That way Nixon could play what had been his best political card since the 1940s: positioning himself as a martyr. He would also have been promoted as a Republican spokesman—where only the previous year he had been a Republican irrelevancy. Right on schedule, the week before the election, Johnson blew his stack against Nixon's Vietnam criticism, delivering what Jules Witcover said was "the most brutal verbal bludgeoning ever administered from the White House by Johnson, or any of the Presidents for that matter, to a leader of the opposition party." The words testified to Nixon's astounding political success. Of the sixty-six candidates Nixon campaigned for, forty-four won; proclaimed the *New York Times*, the "political equivalent of the batting championship for the 1966 campaign season went to former Vice President Richard M. Nixon." In actual fact the Republican sweep had little or nothing to do with Nixon's interventions—the nationwide anti–civil rights backlash was far more the determining factor. But Nixon was brilliantly successful in reaping the credit—and framing it in his preferred terms.[32]

The goat of 1960, 1962, and 1964 was now the leader of the opposition party. By 1967 his only real rival for the nomination was George Romney, the pundits' favorite. But Romney's earnest sincerity proved his downfall against a master dissembler. A TV interviewer asked Romney why his position on Vietnam had changed. Romney replied that his original optimism had been a result of the "brainwashing" the generals and diplomatic corps had given him on his first trip to Vietnam. Metaphorically, the observation was sharp; American officials did badly exaggerate the situa-

[32] Ibid., 96–166.

tion before visiting dignitaries. Politically it was disastrous: it made Romney sound weak, and American officials sound sinister. The remark effectively finished him—even as Nixon first uttered banalities about Vietnam; then pledged "that new leadership will end the war and win the peace in the Pacific"; then refused to say anything else specific, claiming a refusal to interfere with the president's prerogative to make foreign policy.[33]

The race riots in 1967 were worse than in 1966; in 1968, they were joined by the escalating insurrections of antiwar students. The crime rate was skyrocketing. Martin Luther King, Jr., and Robert F. Kennedy were assassinated. Nelson Rockefeller from the left and Ronald Reagan from the right presented themselves as the only Republicans who could bring social peace. At the convention, they both tried to peel off enough Nixon support to deny Nixon a first-ballot victory. The delegates held firm for Nixon, even those who considered Ronald Reagan a saint—held in check by Strom Thurmond, whose loyalty Nixon had further cemented by giving him veto power over his running mate. Nixon's rousing acceptance speech spoke to anxieties over the mounting disorder of the 1960s: he proclaimed that "the first civil right of every American is to be free from domestic violence." His general election commercials, nearly sublimi-

[33] Ibid., 204–5, 235–36.

nal in their jarring, discordant design, attributed the collapse of law and order to Democratic rule.

The campaign was unprecedented in its discipline and tactical shrewdness: he gave only one or two speeches per day, timed for maximal exposure on the evening news. Another crucial component was the carefully choreographed, televised "town hall meeting," invented by media adviser Roger Ailes, later the architect of FOX News. In November, he won a three-way race that included the right-wing demagogue George Wallace. It was the most stupendous political comeback in history. Now, with hardly more than 43 percent of the popular vote, a man whose defining trait was a rage to control would have to govern a nation spiraling out of control.[34]

VI

What kind of president was Richard M. Nixon? On the domestic front, a startlingly indifferent one. He once famously labeled domestic policy "building outhouses in Peoria";[35] he believed such matters took care of themselves, without a president to guide them, and nearly set out to prove it. Later, the laws passed during his adminis-

[34] Joe McGinniss, *The Selling of the President* (New York: Penguin, 1970).

[35] Richard Reeves, *President Nixon: Alone in the White House* (New York: Simon & Schuster, 2001), 33.

tration, and the bills he attempted to pass, earned Nixon a reputation as a sort of liberal. It would be more accurate to say that he took the path of least resistance, and that the conventional policy wisdom of the day was, simply, liberal. He paid closest attention to domestic policy-making when it involved a political constituency he wanted to punish or reward.

He was sold, for example, on adviser Daniel Patrick Moynihan's idea for a guaranteed minimum income to replace the existing welfare system when Moynihan assured him it would wipe out the social welfare bureaucracy, a Democratic political constituency. (In a strategy meeting for the 1972 election, he proposed sabotaging either its passage or its implementation, either way preserving credit for caring about the poor without doing anything of substance at all.) His federal drug control policies could never have survived in our own conservative era: for heroin addicts, they substituted medical treatment for punishment. Nixon's interest in reform was once again political: he hoped rehabilitating heroin addicts would add up to a lower crime rate in time for his 1972 reelection campaign.[36]

His policy preferences also indicated a conflicted eagerness to please opinion-making elites.

[36] Ibid., 45, 636; Michael Massing, *The Fix: Solving the Nation's Drug Problem* (Berkeley and Los Angeles: University of California Press, 2000).

They praised his establishment of an Environmental Protection Agency, launched with an inspiring speech: "the 1970s absolutely must be the years when America pays its debts to the past by reclaiming the purity of its air, its water, and our living environment. It is literally now or never." But he shared another opinion of the issue in an Oval Office meeting with auto executives: that environmentalists wanted to "go back and live like a bunch of damned animals." Throwing conservationists a bone also suited another political purpose: the issue was popular among the same young people who were enraged at him for continuing the Vietnam War. In the end, the EPA was a sort of confidence game. The new agency represented not a single new penny in federal spending for the environment. It did, however, newly concentrate subdepartments previously scattered through the vast federal bureaucracy under a single administrator loyal to the White House—the better to control them.[37]

Here is the other key to understanding Nixon's domestic policy, and much else in the Nixon White House besides: its frequent "reorganizations,"

[37] *Public Papers of the Presidents of the United States: Richard Nixon, 1970* (Washington, DC: U.S. Government Printing Office, 1971), doc. 1, available at http://www.presidency.ucsb.edu/ws/?pid=2446; Bruce J. Schulman, *The Seventies: The Great Shift in American Culture, Society, and Politics* (New York: De Capo Press, 2002), 30; Reeves, *President Nixon*, 238.

which were actually an argument about executive power—that it should be increased, and controlled directly from the Oval Office. His Domestic Policy Council, for example, established his first year, represented a power-grab from cabinet agencies and other independent bureaucracies; its leadership would fall to his number one political enforcer, John Ehrlichman. A reconfiguration of the entire executive branch followed in his second year. Its not-so-innocent intent was suggested by the fact that its advisory council worked in secret, incinerating their trash in "burn bags" every night. The Interstate Commerce Commission, the Civil Aeronautics Board, the Federal Maritime Administration, the Federal Communications Commission, and the Securities and Exchange Commission were among the bureaucracies slated for merger, fragmentation, reduction, or abolition. Many bipartisan governing boards led by officials with fixed statutory terms Nixon sought to replace with White House agencies with chairmen serving at the pleasure of the president, without senatorial confirmation, their duties deliberately unspecified. When Nixon quietly submitted the plan to Congress, and Congress took no action within sixty days, he announced that Congress's Inaction allowed his bureaucratic coup to take effect unilaterally.[38]

[38] Ibid., 98–99, 230; Jonathan Schell, *The Time of Illusion* (New York: Alfred A. Knopf, 1975), 103–4; John W. Dean, *Blind*

The domestic issue that commanded the closest attention in the White House followed upon his pledges to Strom Thurmond. Richard Nixon had attended law school in North Carolina, where he had learned, in certain company, to refer to the Civil War as the "War between the States." When it had been the Republican fashion, he had backed federal civil rights legislation. But he also, his chief of staff Bob Haldeman's diaries revealed, believed in the genetic inferiority of blacks. His campaign promise to Southern Republicans to waylay federal civil rights enforcement was honored via a complex political pas de deux: public pronouncements about desegregation and equal opportunity alongside sub rosa bureaucratic sabotage, his true intentions signaled to Southern conservatives with his federal judicial appointees.[39]

Then, his strangest domestic initiative came down like a thunderclap. As the 1972 election year approached, 73 percent disapproved of his handling of the economy. Inflation was pinioning the middle class; the stock market was tanking. The Democrats had a proposed solution on the table: a freeze on wages and prices. The president, over and over, said he would never ask Congress for such a foolhardy thing. The Democrats, think-

---

Ambition: The White House Years (New York: Simon & Schuster, 1976), 24.

[39] Brodie, *Richard Nixon*, 526; Reeves, *President Nixon*, 110; Perlstein, *Nixonland*, 362, 421, 459–60, 463–68.

ing themselves clever, granted the president power to impose the freeze unilaterally; that way, they could accuse him of being callous and hard-hearted when he did not. They misjudged the shallowness of Richard Nixon's ideological convictions. In August of 1971 he gathered his economic team for an extraordinary three-day conclave at Camp David and ordered them to engineer both a wage-and-price control package and a radical restructuring of the anchor of the international monetary system—the "gold window," agreed to at Bretton Woods in 1944, that let nations exchange U.S. currency for gold at a fixed rate. Federal Reserve chairman Arthur Burns warned of the perils of loosing the American currency from gold, "*Pravda* would write that this was a sign of the collapse of capitalism." Herb Stein of the Council of Economic Advisers, marveling at the short-term cynicism of the policies they were commanded to effect, said he felt as though they'd been hired as scriptwriters for a TV special. The "image of action" was the important thing, the president told them. Nixon sold the new policy on TV as a rescue of the American economy from "the attacks of international money speculators."

Politically, the reversion to an ugly old Republican isolationism worked famously: 75 percent of the country polled in favor of his "New Economic Policy"; the Dow charted its biggest one-day gain in history.[40] These were not, however, the move's only appeals to Richard Nixon. Since childhood, Nixon had raged against what he could not control. And this was a common denominator of so many of his presidential initiatives, policies, and reorganizations, this "New Economic Policy" among them: the quest for control, even of that which could not be controlled.

VII

Richard Nixon's first bureaucratic reorganization had come during his inauguration parade. He issued National Security Decision Memo 2, which disbanded the group within the State Department that checked and balanced the National Security Council. It heralded an unprecedented concentration of foreign policy deliberation within the White House, where it could be carried out in utter secrecy between himself and his national security adviser Henry Kissinger.[41] Playing the chess game of world diplomacy was the meaning of Nixon's lifetime of sacrifice. It was the reason he had longed to be president in the first place.

No one would have predicted that Nixon and Kissinger would become such close partners. Kissinger, a former Kennedy administration official,

[40] Allen J. Matusow, *Nixon's Economy: Booms, Busts, Dollars, and Votes* (Lawrence: University Press of Kansas, 1998).
[41] Reeves, *President Nixon*, 26.

had been adviser to Nixon's greatest party rival, the Republican liberal Nelson Rockefeller. He was Jewish, an intellectual, a Harvard professor—all types that Nixon sorely distrusted. But Kissinger resembled his boss in important respects: he was a brilliant striver, always at the edge of respectability, never quite fully integrated into the councils of the elite, ever counting slights from his Establishment patrons. It helped forge a strange intimacy, a love-hate partnership of unusual intensity. Together, they left the Cold War categories of metaphysical good and evil behind them. Their vision of international order was defined instead by metaphors of control: "balance of power," "equilibrium," "structure of peace."[42]

The opportunities Nixon's years out of power provided for study, travel, and reflection freed a powerful mind from the imperatives of demagoguery. He began to look, in what would become a stock Nixon phrase, at the "long view." Communism was no longer monolithic; the Soviet Union was on the verge of strategic parity with the United States and saw China as a rival, not a partner; the booming capitalist economies of Asia would have more to do with checking the spread of revolution in Asia than any American saber

[42] John Judis, *Grand Illusions: Critics and Champions of the American Century* (New York: Farrar, Straus & Giroux, 1992), 190–224.

rattling; you couldn't export American democracy to the Third World anyway. Balancing nations' interests against one another, vouchsafing stability even at the price of apparent moral inconsistency: this now seemed to him the highest good. His belief that what he was doing was idealistic was signaled by his choice of Oval Office furniture—Woodrow Wilson's desk—and his invocation, in describing his plans, of Mahatma Gandhi, his mother's Quaker pacifism, and the Quaker concept of "peace in the center." Kissinger arrived at the same conclusions coming at the problem from the nineteenth-century European tradition of balance-of-power thought. In words Kissinger scripted for Nelson Rockefeller to deliver on the 1968 campaign trail, Kissinger described the goal thus: in "a subtle triangle with Communist China and the Soviet Union, we can ultimately improve our relations with each, as we test the will for peace of both."[43]

The rhetoric of peace coincided with manifest cruelties in the implementation. In Nixon's 1967 "Asia after Viet Nam" article he spoke of a "U.S. presence" in Indonesia as "a shield behind which the anti-communist forces found the courage and capacity to stage their counter-coup and, at the final moment, to rescue their country from the Chinese orbit." The "counter-coup," in actual

[43] Ibid., 205.

fact, had been a genocide. The hundreds of thousands of victims included not merely Communists and their families but mere ethnic Chinese. As president, Nixon would have occasion to similarly ignore a genocide, by Pakistan against the breakaway province later known as Bangladesh. It was 1971, and the White House had secretly "tilted" toward Pakistan in its conflict with India. America was officially neutral in the conflict. But Pakistan's dictator Yahya Khan was a crucial go-between in Kissinger's ongoing negotiations of an alliance with China. Wrenching the globe into a more peaceful "balance" could be a damned dirty business.[44]

The opening to China was, if nothing else, an awesome diplomatic accomplishment. It is impossible to overstate the intensity of America's previous efforts to isolate the nation that had shocked the world by "going Communist" in 1949. A "kitchen debate" in China was unimaginable; as the diplomatic historian Margaret MacMillan relates, "In the early 1960s, when a Chinese classical opera company came to Toronto, the American authorities announced that any American citizens who bought tickets were violating American law." Nixon called his trip to China in February of 1972—significantly, an election year—"the week that changed the world." And

[44] Christopher Hitchens, *The Trial of Henry Kissinger* (New York: Verso, 2001), 44–71.

among the cascading diplomatic consequences of this game-changing development was his visit, several months later, to the Soviet Union, which yielded more tangible results: a Strategic Arms Limitation Treaty, an antiballistic missile treaty, a billion-dollar trade deal.[45]

He fared less successfully in another overriding strategic objective: persuading these two great sponsors of Communist revolution to pressure their North Vietnamese client to end the war. The effort failed because its premises were flawed: for all his foreign policy vision, Nixon could never get beyond the Cold War cliché that China and Russia exercised control over the Communist insurgencies everywhere. But Chinese and Russian sponsorship was only a contributing, never the determinate, factor. The stubborn misunderstanding resembled the account, in his book *Six Crises*, of the mob attacks on him in South America. He figured it as the conspiracy of beady-eyed agitators in communication with Moscow. In reality, Latin Americans—and Vietnamese—had perfectly organic reasons for violent rage at the United States, reasons far beyond Nixon's power to control: America wished to treat them both like semicolonial spheres of influence.

For Richard Nixon's international vision, Vietnam served as a persistent irritant. Early in his

[45] Margaret MacMillan, *Nixon and Mao: The Week That Changed the World* (New York: Random House, 2007).

second year as president, Nixon delivered to Congress what was dubbed a "State of the World" message. The "First Annual Report to Congress on Foreign Policy" was an awesome intellectual achievement, a sweeping one-hundred-page geostrategic survey with sections on every corner of the globe and considerations of every piece on the international chessboard, some eight pages on Africa policy alone. The rather short discussion of Vietnam looked almost like an afterthought, coming more than fourteen thousand words into the document. It was Asia *after* Vietnam, after all, that he was interested in shaping. But it was Vietnam that consumed ever greater drafts of his attention, and Vietnam, he knew, that would define his legacy.[46]

Many who voted for him in 1968 had done so because they thought they had heard in his campaign's fog of words a promise to end the war. Hard upon his inauguration, doves in both parties urged him to seize the opportunity, as George Aiken, ranking Republican on the Senate Foreign Relations Committee famously put it, to "declare victory and go home." This Nixon chose not to do. Instead he devised an interlocking political and military strategy that combined periodic

[46] *Public Papers of the Presidents of the United States: Richard Nixon, 1970* (Washington, DC: U.S. Government Printing Office, 1971), doc. 45, available at http://www.presidency.ucsb.edu/ws/?pid=2835.

drawdowns of U.S. forces in South Vietnam (from 553,000 at his inauguration to 152,000 by election year 1972) with escalating, and often savagely unpredictable, bombing of North Vietnam. The idea was to intimidate North Vietnam into agreeing to peace terms favorable to the United States. It did not succeed. Publicly, Nixon steadfastly maintained that national honor depended on not abandoning the effort to stand up an independent South Vietnamese government in Saigon, savaging the patriotism of all who said otherwise—while privately, Nixon and Kissinger told intimates that an independent South Vietnam was impossible, and worked on a peace deal to merely hold it together for a temporary "decent interval" following the American withdrawal. That way, Nixon could say he had not lost the Vietnam War. The terms eventually arrived at were no better than the ones on the table in 1968—at the cost of 25,000 more American lives.[47]

He was, at any rate, sorely distracted. The rage for control had so diseased his White House that by the spring of 1973 the Oval Office was consumed by attempts to keep the president's closest associates, and possibly even the president, from going to jail.

[47] "Aiken Suggests U.S. Say It Has Won War," *New York Times*, October 20, 1966; Larry Berman, *No Peace, No Honor: Nixon, Kissinger, and Betrayal in Vietnam* (New York: Touchstone, 2002).

VIII

What was Watergate? The word came to refer not to a single event, but to a cascade of revelations that came forth when Congress and the press began investigating a single event: the June 1972 break-in of Democratic National Committee headquarters at the Watergate Hotel. The revelations—what his former attorney general and 1972 campaign manager, who would go to jail for them, called the "White House horrors"—traced back practically to the onset of his first term. Were they a mere epiphenomenon, as his defenders argue, to Nixon's presidency and career? Horrors dated back to the beginning of his presidency are hard to see as flowing from anything but qualities essential to Nixon.

On Nixon's 116th day in the White House, Henry Kissinger arranged for the FBI to wiretap three members of his own NSC staff, and also the secretary of defense's senior military assistant. Secrecy and bureaucratic containment constituted a central principle of their diplomatic method, and the *New York Times* had just reported their secret bombing in Cambodia. Then Nixon arranged for a bugging through entirely extralegal channels, recruiting a retired policeman from the New York City Red Squad attached to the White House staff to tap the phone of one of the nation's most distinguished columnists, Joseph Kraft. Kraft was friends with Kissinger, and Nixon wanted to know what his right-hand man was up to. Which was only fair: for his part, Kissinger was exploring channels to spy on Nixon. A culture of surveillance, flowing from the rage to control, was endemic to this White House.[48]

The culture of surveillance flowed, too, from principles Nixon first enunciated in a prize-winning 1929 schoolboy speech, "Our Privileges under the Constitution," reenunciated by Nixon to his dying day: as he put it in his maiden House speech in 1947, "the rights of free speech and free press do not carry with them the right to advocate the destruction of the very Government which protects the freedom of an individual to express his views." America was at war in Vietnam, part of a global Cold War; the Americans who opposed it were no better than fifth column sappers; "hundreds, perhaps thousands, of Americans—mostly under 30—are determined to destroy our society," explained a memo from one of the president's favorite staffers, a former army intelligence officer named Tom Charles Huston. By the end of its first year, the administration had one hundred undercover officers compiling dossiers on organizations like the NAACP, the ACLU, and the Southern Christian Leadership Conference. The

[48] Anthony Lukas, *Nightmare: The Underside of the Nixon Years* (New York: Viking, 1976), 44–52, 64–65.

CIA infiltrated antiwar organizations. The Department of Health, Education, and Welfare kept a blacklist of antiwar scientists. An entire unit of the Internal Revenue Service was chartered—in a locked, soundproof room in the IRS basement—to harass them.[49]

The crusade for control extended into the electoral realm, motivated by that other Nixonian principle: that the making and execution of foreign policy was the prerogative solely of the Oval Office. By the middle of 1970, antiwar senators were introducing bills to defund the war. Efforts to defeat them were too important to leave to the Republican Party (indeed some of the most influential antiwar senators were in the Republican Party). So the White House financed an entire campaign apparatus to beat antiwar senators, organized out of a Georgetown basement. Rich men and corporations seeking favors from the White House were all but ordered to offer up donations outside the conventional campaign finance system. White House lawyers were convinced this was legal, since disclosure requirements didn't apply to donations made "in" the

[49] Brodie, *Richard Nixon*, chapter 14; Reeves, *President Nixon*, 235–36; Kutler, *Wars of Watergate*, 97, 105; Schell, *Time of Illusion*, 114; Karl E. Campbell, "Senator Sam Ervin and the Army Spy Scandal of 1970–1971: Balancing National Security and Civil Liberties in a Free Society," Charlotte-Mecklenburg Historic Landmarks Commission, http://www.cmhpf.org/senator%20sam%20ervin.htm; Lukas, *Nightmare*, 22.

District of Columbia. But also by this time, the White House had already drawn up plans to consider what Huston stressed were "clearly illegal" breaking and entering as a component in the crusade for control.[50]

Nixon acted not despite the Silent Majority he described as so pure and decent, but, in a sense, on their behalf, even at their request. His paranoia and dread were their own; the antiwar insurgents, the hippies, the Black Panthers, were taking over. The test was the 1970 off-year elections, for which Nixon and Vice President Spiro Agnew crisscrossed the nation fulminating about the preservation of civilization against the barbarians. They thought they could not lose. What happened was: they lost. This was the trauma—the loss of control—that many judge the point of no return on the road to Watergate. An internal White House unit was established to "plug leaks"—the "Plumbers." In the middle of 1971 they became the operational arm of a presidential obsession: destroying the man, Daniel Ellsberg, who had leaked a massive Pentagon study exposing America's failures in Vietnam. Nixon responded like a mad sorcerer, convinced that the "Pentagon Papers" was but the latest chapter in a feckless Establishment's endless war against him. Nixon begged the men around him to firebomb the Brookings Institution, certain

[50] Reeves, *President Nixon*, 153, 231, 244–45.

that the liberal think tank was hording secret intelligence that could bring down the government-in-exile conspiring against him. The Plumbers were sent to Los Angeles to break into Daniel Ellsberg's psychiatrist's office. These were points of no return. All of it was justified in the name of protecting national security, which the president had come to identify as coextensive with his own person, like a monarch: "if the President does it," he explained his thinking in a 1977 interview, "it's not illegal."[51]

Nixon had a favorite associate, Chuck Colson, his constant companion in mad schemes like this. Colson reflected to the president that summer: "I have not yet thought through all the subtle ways in which we can keep the Democratic Party in a constant state of civil warfare." As election year 1972 approached, that project of degrading the opposition party's political capabilities, to deliver up a November mandate for a Nixon second term, became the Oval Office's consuming passion. Any imaginable Democratic presidency, the president justified to himself, would be "extremely dangerous internationally." And so, funded by more secret slush funds, two separate teams fanned out to states to sabotage candidates vying for the Demo-

[51] Perlstein, *Nixonland*, 578–84, 592–97; David Frost, *"I Gave them a Sword": Behind the Scenes of the Nixon Interviews* (New York: Morrow, 1978).

cratic presidential nomination. Their techniques were fiendish: fake invitations to nonexistent campaign events; smearing letters sent to voters; fake ties "established" to radical groups—all carefully designed to make it look as if they originated from other Democratic campaigns. Only one contender was left alone: George McGovern, the most left-wing viable candidate. One aim of the sabotage strategy was to strengthen his candidacy vis-à-vis the others, because Nixon thought he'd be the one easiest to beat in the general election.[52]

Another of Nixon's dirty tricks in 1972 was bribing George Wallace out of running for president as a Democrat instead of as a third-party candidate. That kept the divisive issue of busing in the forefront of the Democratic primaries, ratcheting up the civil warfare yet further. When Wallace was paralyzed in an assassination attempt in May, the Democratic race was still competitive between McGovern and Hubert Humphrey. Now the crucial question was how the delegates he won would be distributed. The decision rested with Democratic National Committee chair Lawrence O'Brien, a longtime Nixon bête noir and Kennedy family retainer. That may have been one

[52] Bruce Oudes, ed., *From: The President. Richard Nixon's Secret Files* (New York: HarperCollins, 1989), 182–84; Matusow, *Nixon's Economy*, 84; Perlstein, *Nixonland*, 623–24, 629–33, 635; Lukas, *Nightmare*, 165.

of the more important motives for the bugging of O'Brien's office in the Watergate for intelligence on Democratic political activities. The bugging, however, proved unsuccessful. The burglary team returned to fix the problem on June 16, but this time they were caught. The president was protected from knowing the precise details of such operations; he served more as their inspiration and goad. Following the arrest of the Watergate burglars, however, he was quickly brought up to speed. His response was to direct, with cunning and gusto, a cover-up of White House ties to the crime, and a strategy to obstruct all investigations. It worked long enough to secure Nixon's landslide reelection. But once Congress turned to the investigation with subpoena power, Watergate became what the Hiss case had been from 1948 to 1950—a gripping multiyear national soap opera, only this time with Nixon as the hunted instead of the hunter.[53]

Nixon's presidency limped to its denouement by way of a grim paradox: his lieutenants were shown conducting illicit operations of such high stakes and complexity that only a senior official would have supervised them. But the more senior the official who was suborned into taking respon-

[53] Perlstein, *Nixonland*, 631–32; Lukas, *Nightmare*, 195–231; Kutler, *Wars of Watergate*.

sibility, the further he stood to fall; and the better he knew the error of trusting this president to protect him. John Dean, the White House counselor charged by the president with coordinating the cover-up, broke in June of 1973, testifying in minute detail of the president's complicity in crimes to the Senate Watergate committee. At first, it was merely his word against Nixon's. Then the nation was shocked to learn that Nixon had recorded nearly every word uttered in his Oval Office on voice-activated tapes: hoist on his own petard by the very obsession with control that defined him. By the summer of 1974, keeping these tapes from congressional investigators became the pitiful essence of his ruined presidency. Richard Nixon could not survive the public's naked confrontation with Richard Nixon. The Supreme Court ruled the tapes belonged to the public, not to him personally, on July 24, 1974. He resigned fifteen days later ahead of certain Senate conviction on three articles of impeachment.[54]

The next day, August 8, 1974, he gave a speech to his White House staff that provided a way for his diehard defenders to process the awful previous months. It was the same story he'd been telling since he founded the salt-of-the-earth Orthogoni-

[54] Rick Perlstein, "The Unraveling: The Tale of the New Nixon Tapes," *Slate*, November 26, 1997, http://www.slate.com/id/3028/.

ans to do battle with the snooty, condescending Franklins. He rehearsed his background: his father was "a streetcar motorman first, and then he was a farmer, and then he had a lemon ranch. It was the poorest lemon ranch in California, I can assure you." "My mother," he said, "was a saint." He himself had chosen public service, and had not enriched himself—for there was something "far more important than money. It is a cause bigger than yourself. It is the cause of making this the greatest nation in the world." He advertised his humility: "I am not educated, but I do read books."

He also included the following strange detail. "Nobody will ever write a book, probably, about my mother." It was a reference to men not so humble, men born with silver spoons in their mouths—men who looked down on you and me. Rose Kennedy, matriarch of the clan, had just come out with an autobiography, and it was the talk of the opinion-making elites. Then he repeated it: "Yes, she will have no books written about her." Because we are not Kennedys, they won't cut us a break: in his self-pity, he couldn't resist an oblique swipe at the well-born, the snooty, the sophisticates—his enemies. He seemed almost to blame them him for his fate: "Always remember, others may hate you, but those who hate you don't win unless you hate them, and then you destroy yourself." They had forced him to hate them. They had not let his sagacity and good intentions come to the fore. From that, all else followed. If gold rust, what shall iron do?[55]

IX

Once more, it was not the end. It wasn't long before Richard Nixon was submitting himself to one more campaign—this one for ex-president, for the right to be deferred to and respected like any other former occupant of the Oval Office. He marketed himself as a foreign policy sage, the man who could take the long view, the guru of peace. Once more, as President Kennedy had once advised him, the vector was writing books. They rolled off the presses at regular intervals, titles like *The Real War* (1980), *Leaders: Profiles and Reminisces of Men Who Have Shaped the Modern World* (1982), *No More Vietnams* (1987), 1999: *Victory without War* (1988), *Seize the Moment: America's Challenges in the One Superpower World* (1992), and, finally, *Beyond Peace* (1994). He carried out, too, another campaign, this one in the courtroom: attempting to keep his White House tapes out of

[55] *Public Papers of the Presidents of the United States: Richard Nixon, 1974* (Washington, DC: U.S. Government Printing Office, 1975), doc. 245, available at http://www.presidency.ucsb.edu/ws/?pid=4325.

the public domain. He spent an estimated five million dollars to do so.

The latter effort failed, though posthumously: two years after Nixon's 1994 death, the National Archives reached a settlement that would eventually bring more than three thousand hours of tapes into the public domain.[56] The former campaign was a very limited success. Historians in a 2000 *Wall Street Journal* canvass ranked him merely "Below Average"—above "Failures" Tyler, Fillmore, and Pierce. Richard Nixon became Ronald Reagan's most frequent outside consultant on foreign afffairs. The notion of Nixon as the last bastion of moderate, even liberal, Republican policy-making took hold; the opening to China is heralded as a masterstroke; even the abuses of power, some believe, have come to pale in comparison to those of George W. Bush, whose devotion to executive secrecy John W. Dean has called, in the title of a book, *Worse Than Watergate*. The word has had the effect of containing his failings in the public mind: if Watergate was bad, everything else must have been better. At Nixon's funeral—after declaring a national day of mourning—President Clinton said as much himself: "May the day of judging President Nixon on anything less than his entire life and career come to a

[56] Stanley Kutler, *Abuse of Power: The New Nixon Tapes* (New York: Free Press, 1997), xiv–xv.

close." Gerald Ford called him "one of the finest, if not the finest, foreign policy presidents of this century." Senator Bob Dole of Kansas, the Republican National Committee chair during Watergate, orated that "the second half of the 20th century will be known as the age of Nixon."[57]

In a sense he surely did not intend, Bob Dole was correct. What Nixon left behind was the very terms of our national self-image: the notion that there are two kinds of Americans. On the one side: Nixon's "Silent Majority," the "non-shouters": the Middle Class, Middle America; the suburban, exurban, and rural coalition who call themselves "value voters," "people of faith," and "patriots"—and who feel themselves condescended to by snobby opinion-making elites. On the other side are the "liberals," the "cosmopolitans," the "intellectuals." They see shouting in opposition to injustice as a higher form of patriotism; they say "live and let live"; they believe having "values" has more to do with a willingness to extend aid to the downtrodden than with where, or whether, you happen to worship—and they look down on the first category as unwitting dupes of feckless elites who exploit sentimental

[57] *Wall Street Journal* Online, "Hail to the Chief: Scholars Rank the Presidents," http://www.opinionjournal.com/hail/; author interview with Richard Reeves; Maureen Dowd, "The 37th President: The Overview; Nixon Buried on Note of Praise and Reconciliation," *New York Times*, April 28, 1994.

pieties to aggrandize their wealth. Both populations are equally, essentially American. And each has learned to consider the other not quite American at all. In that sense, Bob Dole was correct. The argument over Richard Nixon, pro and con, gave us the language for this war. We are living in the Age of Nixon still.

Bibliographic Note

Some of the documents herein are presented in their entirety. Others are excerpts, with the missing portions indicated by ellipses. Many of these excerpted documents, however, can be easily found online in full via Google, including the Frank Gannon interviews (chapter 4), the Checkers speech (chapter 7), the first Kennedy-Nixon debate (chapter 10), the "Last Press Conference" (chapter 11), and the 1968 acceptance speech (chapter 16). Also, every official presidential utterance (chapters 17, 18, 19, 20, 21, 22, 23, 24, 26, 27, 28, 29, and 30) is accessible at http://www.presidency.ucsb.edu. A selection of important transcripts of President Nixon's conversations regarding Watergate and related matters can be found in Stanley Kutler, *Abuse of Power: The New Nixon Tapes* (New York: Free Press, 1997). They can be listened to in full at the National Archives in College Park, Maryland, and all the recordings are slowly being digitized by the Miller Center of Public Affairs at the University of Virginia and made available at http://millercenter.org/index.php/academic/presidentialrecordings/pages/tapes_rmn.

I would be glad to entertain questions at Nixonland@live.com.

Rick Perlstein
Chicago, Illinois

I. Youth

1.

From *RN: The Memoirs of Richard Nixon* (1978)

The opening passages of Nixon's memoir put several Nixonian traits on full display: first and most neglected, that Nixon was an outstanding storyteller, a quality that explains his consistent ability to connect with ordinary Americans despite his oft-remarked personal awkwardness. Second is the surprising quality of self-revelation on frequent display in his autobiographical reflections ("My first conscious memory is of running": here is the essential Nixonian quality—restless striving). There are the notes of self-pity: the deux ex machina that robbed his family of "unlimited opportunity"; the scar that kept him from parting his hair in the vogue of the day. Finally there is the deep psychological imprint that the modesty of his upbringing made on him, combined with the cosmopolitan yearning of the devoted National Geographic *reader who even then longs for worlds to conquer.*

I was born in a house my father built. My birth on the night of January 9, 1913, coincided with a record-breaking cold snap in our town of Yorba Linda, California. Yorba Linda was a farming community of 200 people about thirty miles from

Los Angeles, surrounded by avocado and citrus groves and barley, alfalfa, and bean fields.

For a child the setting was idyllic. In the spring the air was heavy with the rich scent of orange blossoms. And there was much to excite a child's imagination: glimpses of the Pacific Ocean to the west, the San Bernardino Mountains to the north, a 'haunted house' in the nearby foothills to be viewed with awe and approached with caution—and a railroad line that ran about a mile from our house.

In the daytime I could see the smoke from the steam engines. Sometimes at night I was awakened by the whistle of a train, and then I dreamed of far-off places I wanted to visit someday. My brothers and I played railroad games, taking the parts of engineers and conductors. I remember the thrill of talking to Everett Barnum, the Santa Fe Railroad engineer who lived in our town. All through grade school my ambition was to become a railroad engineer. . . .

2.

Two letters (1923 and 1924)

The ten-year-old Nixon's letter to his mother addressed to "My Dear Master" and signed "Your good dog, Richard" (it was composed for a school assignment to write a letter in the voice of a pet) has long proved a fascination for psychobiographers, with its fantastic images of unearned persecutions. His letter ten weeks later to the conservative big-city daily his family took and which he devoured foreshadows another Nixonian trait: an awkward willingness to grovel before high-status elders to elevate his station in life.

Nov. 12, 1923

My Dear Master:
The two dogs that you left with me are very bad to me. Their dog, Jim, is very old and he will never talk or play with me. One Saturday the boys went hunting. Jim and myself went with them. While going through the woods one of the boys triped and fell on me. I lost my temper and bit him. He kiked me in the side and we started on. While we were walking I saw a black round thing in a tree. I hit it with my paw. A swarm of black thing came out of it. I felt a pain all over. I started to run and

as both of my eyes were swelled shut I fell into a pond. When I got home I was very sore. I wish you would come home right now.

Your good dog
Richard

• • •

Times, Office K, Box 240
January 24, 1924

Dear Sir:
Please consider me for the position of office boy mentioned in the Times paper. I am eleven years of age and I am in the Sixth grade of the East Whittier grammar school.

I am very willing to work and would like the money for a vacation trip. I am willing to come to your office at any time and I will accept any pay offered. My address is Whittier boulevard and Leffingwell road. The phone number is 5274. For reference you can see, Miss Flowers principal of the East Whittier School. Hoping that you will accept me for service, I am

Yours truly,
Richard M. Nixon

3.

"Our Privileges under the Constitution" (1929)

The argument of Nixon's winning entry in a schoolboy elocution contest appeared almost identically in his maiden congressional speech in 1947 ("the rights of free speech and free press do not carry with them the right to advocate the destruction of the very Government which protects the freedom of an individual to express his views"), and again in 1965, when Nixon attacked a college professor for announcing he welcomed a Communist victory in Vietnam. In a career full of ideological inconsistencies, it may have been Nixon's most consistent position: beware subversives exploiting the First Amendment to undermine American civilization itself. The claim that civilization must be thus protected, even at the expense of what a sixteen-year-old describes here as merely provisional constitutional "privileges," provided one of the rationalizations for Watergate, which began after Nixon became convinced that an intellectual named Daniel Ellsberg had conspired to subvert the nation by leaking the Pentagon's secret history of the Vietnam War.

Ladies and Gentlemen:

For countless centuries man has aspired to freedom. The pages of history are replete with the stories of men and women who have given their lives that they and their posterity might have the blessings of freedom. When we consider the development of our own liberties, we recall the stirring deeds of our English ancestors; how they secured from the unwilling hands of their despotic kings those priceless guaranties of freedom—the Magna Charta and the Bill of Rights. We remember with pride how our American forefathers, being refused the rights granted by their charters, and oppressed by a despotic king, defied one of the mightiest nations in existence, and proved victorious in the struggle that followed. Then we think of the steps those men made to establish their newborn liberties in a lasting government: how they at first failed to obtain the desired results by the Articles of Confederation, but how, undaunted, they finally produced a document that has withstood the trials of nearly a century and a half—our Constitution.

Today we are receiving the benefits of that freedom for which so many of our forefathers paid the supreme sacrifice. Let us consider those benefits—our privileges under the Constitution.

The chief desire of man is that his life and personal liberty may be well protected. While our forefathers were struggling for freedom, one of their grievances was that a man, accused of a crime, was not always given a fair chance to prove himself innocent, and was thus often unjustly punished. Therefore the framers of the Constitution provided for the highest type of justice. No citizen of the United States can be tried for a capital crime without first being indicted by a grand jury. He may obtain counsel and witnesses. He is not compelled to testify against himself as in times past, nor is any evidence obtained by compulsion. A great number of innocent persons would have been saved from ignominious death if such rights could have been had in times past. These privileges for trial mean much to us, for they protect us from unjust accusations and punishments. Let us safeguard them by protecting the Constitution which insures them.

Many of our forefathers came to America because they had been refused the privilege of free worship. They left behind them nations burdened with horrors of religious wars caused by the intolerance of men in power toward others with different religious views. The framers of the Constitution wisely provided against such wars in this nation by inserting a clause insuring free worship. We are truly fortunate to have this privilege; but let us not think that, since the Constitution provides for free worship, persons may indulge in religious practices which are debasing to mind and character. Such practices are in direct contrast to the spirit of the Constitution. Rather, in remembrance of those who have given us this privilege, let us protect it and hold it sacred.

During the struggle for freedom, our forefathers were in constant danger of punishment for exercising the rights of freedom of speech and freedom of the press. Again the cause of their danger was the intolerance of men in power toward others with different views. The framers of the Constitution provided that we, their descendants, need not fear to express our sentiments as they did. Yet the question arises: How much ground do these privileges cover? There are some who use them as a cloak for covering libelous, indecent, and injurious statements against their fellowmen. Should the morals of this nation be offended and polluted in the name of freedom of speech or freedom of the press? In the words of Lincoln, the individual can have no rights against the best interests of society. Furthermore there are those who, under the pretense of freedom of speech and freedom of the press have incited riots, assailed our patriotism, and denounced the Constitution itself. They have used Constitutional privileges to protect the very act by which they wished to destroy the Constitution. Consequently laws have justly been provided for punishing those who abuse their Constitutional privileges—laws which do not limit these privileges, but which provide that they may not be instrumental in destroying the Constitution which insures them. We must obey these laws, for they have been passed for our own welfare.

If we should delve into the histories of great nations, we should see that in the past the common people have been forced to serve and support the nobility; that they had been given no chance to gain power; and that they had had scarcely any part in the government. Contrast such governments with our own.

In the United States, the people themselves are the rulers. Gone are the days of inequality and servitude. We derive our powers from the privilege of suffrage. Let us see how it has been established in the Constitution. When this document was first adopted, the privilege of suffrage was held by all free male citizens. Three quarters of a century later the curse of slavery was removed forever from this nation, and the ballot was extended to all men regardless of race or color. In our own time this privilege has been fully established by the Constitution, and has been extended to all citizens regardless of sex. But do we fully appreciate this privilege? Does it seem right that, in the presidential elections of 1920 and 1924, little over fifty percent of the eligible voting public went to the polls, and that in our last election little over sixty-five percent cast their ballots? Can those millions of American people who each year fail to go to the polls be called true American citizens? We must become educated to a higher appreciation of the privilege of suffrage, for the destiny of this nation is guided by the American people alone. To use the ballot is the citizen's duty to himself, to his fellowmen, and to his country. It is his debt to those innumerable patriots whose sacrifices have made possible his present day privileges.

In times past the right to hold office was given only to those of the nobility, we however, have our Lincolns and our Jacksons—men who needed only a chance to prove their worth, that they might rise to the highest office in the land. Truly it is a great privilege to hold office, but it is also a great responsibility. The office holder is elected by his fellowmen, who expect him to represent them wisely and justly. It is his duty to give his services willingly, no matter how insignificant the position; to perform his work to the best of his ability; and to defend, maintain, and uphold the Constitution.

By these two political privileges, of suffrage and of holding office, the American citizen is a ruler more powerful than any king. Let us not be unworthy of our great power.

Fellow citizens, when we consider all our privileges, we see that we are a most fortunate people to be living under the rule of a Constitution which has been built upon the very rock of freedom. Our forefathers have given their lives that this Constitution might live, that we, their descendants might enjoy its privileges. It is our duty to protect this precious document, to obey its laws, to hold sacred its mighty principles, that our descendants might have those priceless heritages—Our Privileges under the Constitution.

4.

From the Frank Gannon interviews (1983)

Richard Nixon sat for thirty hours of videotaped interviews with his friend and former employee Frank Gannon. In this excerpt, Nixon describes his exclusion from Whittier College's single social club, the Franklins, and how he and his fellow outcasts subsequently chartered their own, the Orthogonians.

Frank Gannon: What were the "four b's"?

Nixon: Well, the four b's—that had to do with a little society which I suppose some would call a fraternity. Whittier College did not have fraternities. They didn't believe in elitism at all, but they did have societies, because people do get together. And when I went to Whittier in my freshman year, the men's society on campus was called the Franklin Society. And those were the sort of—frankly, the better-off students, the ones that had a little more than the rest, and so forth and so on. And an indication of how well off they were was that for the student yearbook they had their pictures taken in tuxedoes.

Dean Triggs, who was a sophomore when I was a freshman, had spent his first year at Colorado

College. He had been a member of a fraternity there, Beta Theta Phi, a very good one. And when he came in, and he saw the Franklins there—and Dean was on the football team as I was and so forth—he said, "Let's start another society." So he did, and those who joined the society, all the charter members, were football players, or in athletics one way or another.

And I wrote the constitution for it, and I wrote the—I wrote the song for it. Dean, however, gave us the ideas about its initiation, which was a horrible thing, I thought. He also gave us the slogan of the society, écrasons l'infâme, which, as you recall, Voltaire used to say that, "Stamp out evil." Whatever that could mean at that period in our lives. And then these—the—it was—the four b's stood for beans, brains, brawn, and bowels. Now the bowels, of course, were guts for the football players; the brains, we were all, we were all students; the brawn, we were going to be strong; the beans was that in those Depression years, every week we used to get together for a feed. We didn't have meat, so we had beans. Now and then we'd throw a little hamburger in it. So we had bean feeds every week, and we did eat beans. . . .

[W]e would have the Orthogonian Men's Square, and we'd all sit around and we'd have a 'knock and boost' session, and you'd go right around the table, and there'd be about twenty-five of us, and each fellow'd get up and say, "I have a boost for this guy for—and I have a knock for him, 'cause I didn't like what he did in—in the classroom the other day," or, "He's been makin' eyes at my girl," or what have you. I thought it was—it just really turned me off. I couldn't do it. I've never knocked anybody, incidentally, at that one. I could give them a boost, but what I didn't like was the—the fact that it was such an invasion of privacy. I—I know—I know these days that there is the proper therapy for alcoholism, for psychiatric problems, et cetera, et cetera to have this laying on a couch or discussing all these things, and so forth and so on. No way for me. I could never do it.

II. Congress

5.

"The Hiss Case—A Lesson for the American People" (January 26, 1950)

In this epochal 1950 special order House speech Nixon didn't just narrate the Hiss case. He fixed it as a morality tale not merely about the struggle against Communism, but about the arrogant fecklessness of the eastern Establishment, more concerned for their status than for the safety of the nation. It was an argument about social class: "The tragedy of this case is that men like Alger Hiss who come from good families, are graduates of our best schools, and are awarded the highest honors in Government service, find the Communist ideology more attractive than American democracy."

Two weeks later, Senator Joseph McCarthy borrowed extensive passages of Nixon's speech outright in his famous address in Wheeling, West Virginia, in which he stole from Nixon the title as the nation's most prominent "Red" hunter.

Mr. Speaker, this is the first time I have imposed upon the membership by asking for a special order for the purpose of addressing the House. I have done so on this occasion because I feel that I have a solemn responsibility, both as a member of the Committee on Un-American Activities and as a

Member of this House to lay certain facts concerning the case which led to the trial and conviction of Alger Hiss for perjury before the Members of the House and the American people.

This case and the implications which arise from it involve considerations which affect the very security of this Republic. This Nation cannot afford another Hiss case. It is essential therefore that we recognize the seriousness of the crime involved, the extent and scope of the conspiracy of which Mr. Hiss was a member, the reasons for failure to bring that conspiracy to light until it was too late to prosecute those involved for the crime they had committed, and the positive steps which we can and must take now to guard against such a situation in the future.

In discussing the case, I shall go into some detail, particularly with respect to that period during which the Committee on Un-American Activities was conducting its investigation and its hearing. I believe that a presentation of these details will enable the Members of the House to reach their own conclusions as to what lessons the American people should learn from this tragic experience. . . .

The story began in 1948, on July 31. On that date the Committee on Un-American Activities began its investigation into Communist espionage within the Federal Government. The witness who appeared that day was Elizabeth Bentley. She testified before the committee for several hours during the day, both in executive session and in public session, and she named a number of Government employees who, during the war, she said, turned over to her confidential and secret Government documents. That testimony had a tremendous impact upon official Washington. There were charges and countercharges, denials that the testimony was true. The committee, as a result, called in a number of the individuals Miss Bentley had named and gave them the opportunity to give their side of the case. Some of them persisted in their denials, but the majority of them, when they came before the committee, followed the line of refusing to answer any questions covering Miss Bentley's charges on the ground that an answer that they would give to the question might tend to incriminate them.

On August 3, just a week after Miss Bentley appeared, the committee called before it a witness we thought might be able to corroborate some of her testimony. Up to this time all we had was Miss Bentley's testimony about the espionage ring she said she worked with. No other member of the ring had broken, and consequently it was only her word against the word of some who denied the charges and others who refused to answer questions on the basis of self-incrimination.

I mention this because the charge has been made on several occasions that Mr. Chambers on his own initiative came before the Committee on

Un-American Activities and asked for the opportunity to testify so that he could smear Mr. Hiss in a public forum. That was not the case. The committee went to Mr. Chambers. We had learned that he had made charges many years ago, in 1939, to the officials of this Government concerning Communist activities among Federal employees in the period between 1934 and 1937. Consequently we supenaed him to appear before the committee for the purpose of seeing whether he could corroborate Miss Bentley's testimony in any respect.

This was the first time any member of our committee had had the opportunity to see Mr. Chambers. We saw before us a man who was not, at first appearance, a very impressive witness. He spoke in a very low voice. On several occasions the chairman had to ask him to raise his voice so that members of the committee could understand what he said. But the charges he made were of a most serious nature.

He said he had been a Communist until 1938 and that from 1934 to 1937 it was his assigned duty to work with a ring of Communist Party members who held positions in the Government. He named some of the people who were members of the ring. He named others at later sessions of the committee, when we went into the matter in greater detail.

Among the people he named that day were Alger Hiss and Donald Hiss, who had held high positions in the State Department; Lee Pressman, the former general counsel of the CIO; Nathan Witt, the former secretary of the National Labor Relations Board; John Abt, a former Labor Department attorney, Henry Collins, who was with the State Department, and Harry Dexter White, an Assistant Secretary of the Treasury at the time he left Government service.

I mention only a few of the names because it serves to give you an indication of the importance of the people Mr. Chambers said were members of his group.

The day after Mr. Chambers testified we received a request from Mr. Alger Hiss to appear before the committee for the purposes of denying the charges. Let us lay the stage for Mr. Hiss's appearance.

Mr. Hiss was the president of the Carnegie Foundation for International Peace. You know his phenomenal record in Government service. I do not need to go into that. Mr. Chambers had charged that Mr. Hiss had been a Communist between 1934 and 1938. He had denied the charges and asked for the opportunity to be heard. The committee granted him that opportunity.

Mr. Hiss appeared before the committee for the first time on August 5. He said in effect two things: First, that he was not and had never been a Communist; and second, and this was his first mistake, that he had never known a man by the name of Whittaker Chambers. When shown a picture of Chambers he said he could not recognize it as anybody he might have known.

I remember he looked up at the chairman, who was presiding that day, Mr. Mundt, of South Dakota, now a distinguished Member of the other body, and said, "If this is a picture of Mr. Chambers he is not particularly unusual looking. He looks like a lot of people. I might even mistake him for the chairman of this committee."

At the conclusion of Mr. Hiss' testimony that day, those of you who were there, and I see a number of you in the Chamber today, will remember the great impression he made upon the committee, upon the press, and upon those who were there as spectators. I would say that 90 percent of those who were in the committee room were convinced that Mr. Hiss was telling the truth. They were convinced that he was not a Communist, and they were further convinced that he was telling the truth when he said that he did not know Mr. Chambers.

Immediately after the public hearing the committee went into an executive session, and at that point the Hiss-Chambers investigation was almost dropped. It was almost dropped because most of the members of the committee felt that Mr. Chambers must have either been mistaken as to the identity of the man he had named, or that he had concocted this story in order to destroy Mr. Hiss because of some sinister motive that had not been apparent when he had testified before us.

Mr. Stripling, the chief investigator of the committee, and I had some doubts. I do not say that to indicate that we had any greater ability to analyze the evidence than the other members who attended the hearing. But by reason of certain conduct of Mr. Hiss on the stand, we felt at least that we should investigate further to determine whether or not Mr. Hiss or Mr. Chambers was lying on the critical issues. We knew we could not establish which man was telling the truth on the issue of whether Mr. Hiss was a Communist because unless we could get somebody else to break who was a member of the same ring, it was simply Mr. Chambers' word against Mr. Hiss'. But on the question of whether or not Mr. Hiss knew Mr. Chambers, that certainly was a simple issue of fact the truth or falsity of which could be established by corroborative evidence. As a result, we did a very simple and obvious thing. We went to New York City on August 7, subpenaed Chambers and put him under a grueling cross-examination for a period of 3 hours, during which time we went into the most intimate details of his relationship with Mr. Hiss.

I point this out because this was the first time that such an investigation had been made, despite the fact that it was back in 1939 that Mr. Chambers had made these same charges and had made them in even greater detail to Mr. Berle, who was then in the State Department.

As we asked Mr. Chambers these questions we got forthright answers, one after another, and when he completed his testimony we came to the conclusion that either Mr. Chambers knew Mr. Hiss, or that he had made a very careful study of Mr. Hiss's life and as a result of that study, had been able to answer the questions. To give you an indication of how thoroughly we went into the matter, these are some of the questions we asked:

"What was his nickname?

"Did they have any pets?

"What was his hobby?

"What kind of car did he have?

"What houses did he live in while you knew him?"

I remember one question particularly. When we asked what Mr. Hiss' hobby was, Chambers said:

"Mr. and Mrs. Hiss were both amateur ornithologists. They used to get up early in the morning to go to Glen Echo, out to the canal, to observe birds. I recall once they saw to their great excitement, a prothonotary warbler."

We knew from that answer alone that one person could not know such intimate details about another unless he had known him some time in his life.

We returned to Washington and began what at the outset seemed to be the almost impossible task of checking the accuracy of the information Mr. Chambers had given us. It was particularly difficult because we could get no assistance whatever from the intelligence agencies of the Government due to the President's freeze order. . . .

We checked the houses where Mr. Hiss had lived. We checked motor-vehicle registrations and transfers. We even checked dog kennels in Georgetown trying to establish the truth or falsity of Chambers' answers.

The story checked out in every detail where corroborative evidence was available. We then concluded that we had enough evidence to ask Mr. Hiss to come before us again and explain if he could how Mr. Chambers could know these things about him.

On August 16 Mr. Hiss came before us again this time in executive session. We went right down the line asking him the very same questions we had asked Mr. Chambers. We got the same answers. So at the conclusion of that testimony we said, "Mr. Hiss, we have asked Mr. Chambers these questions and he has given us the same answers that you have given us. Tell us now how it is possible for a man you do not even know to know these intimate things about you."

Mr. Hiss still had not come to the point where he could or would admit that he had known

Mr. Chambers. But he said he had once known a man by the name of George Crosley, to whom he said he had rented his apartment in Washington early in 1935 and who had welshed on the rent. He had also given him an automobile, ridden to New York with him on one occasion, and Crosley, his wife and child had spent several days in his home with him and Mrs. Hiss. But he did not think Crosley could be Chambers and he did not know Crosley to be a Communist.

The obvious thing to do then was to confront these two men, since we had diametrically opposing stories, and since it was apparent that both men must have known each other, in view of the testimony we had. The confrontation took place in room 1400 of the Commodore Hotel, New York City. I will describe what happened briefly to indicate to you why the committee came to the conclusion that there were some very grave doubts about the story Mr. Hiss had told in his first appearance before the committee on August 5.

We brought Mr. Hiss into the room first and seated him in a chair. We then had a committee investigator bring Mr. Chambers into the room from behind him and had him sit on the sofa opposite Mr. Hiss. During the time Mr. Chambers was entering the room, Mr. Hiss, who had said he would like to see this man who had made these charges against him, stared straight ahead. He did not turn around once to look at Mr. Chambers as he entered the room.

Then we had the two men rise. I said:

"Mr. Hiss, can you identify this man as anybody you have ever known?"

Mr. Hiss said:

"I wonder if you could have him speak."

I asked Mr. Chambers to state his name and his business. Mr. Chambers answered. Mr. Hiss rose from his chair, advanced on Mr. Chambers, and demanded that he open his mouth wider and also go on talking. Mr. Chambers tried to do so and Mr. Hiss raised on tiptoe and peered into his mouth. Then he said:

"Mr. Chairman, was his voice when he testified before the committee pitched in a lower key?"

Mr. McDowell said it was about the same. Mr. Hiss said:

"Would you have him read some more?"

I happened to have handy a copy of *Newsweek* magazine, which I handed to the senior editor of *Time* magazine, and he read from that.

Mr. Hiss then said that Chambers' teeth looked different and that he would not want to identify him as Crosley until he checked further.

I asked Mr. Chambers if he had ever had any work done on his teeth, and he said he had some bridgework done in the front of his mouth.

We thought certainly Mr. Hiss would admit then he had known Mr. Chambers as Crosley. But no. He said:

"I wonder if you could give me the name of the dentist who did this work."

I said:

"Do you mean you would have to have a man's dentist tell you just what he did to his teeth in order to identify him as somebody you once knew?"

At that point Mr. Hiss changed the subject, and eventually, about 30 minutes later, he finally admitted that Chambers was the man that he had once known as Crosley. But he continued to deny that Chambers was known to him as a Communist, or that he was a Communist or that there was anything at all to the charges which Chambers had made.

We returned to Washington and called in Lee Pressman, John Abt, Henry Collins, and Nathan Witt. They all refused to answer questions on the ground of self-incrimination when we asked them if they knew Chambers or Hiss.

On August 25 we brought Chambers and Hiss together again in a public session in Washington. As a result of that public confrontation, public opinion concerning the truth or falsity of the charges which Mr. Chambers had made, began to change. Because of that change Mr. Hiss was placed in a position where he felt he had to vindicate himself.

This is the way he went about it. At the confrontation scene on August 16, in New York City, he had dared Mr. Chambers to make his charges in public so that he could sue him for libel. Mr. Chambers went on a radio program, *Meet the Press*, on August 27. He was asked whether Mr. Hiss was a Communist. Without relying on the perfect right that he had to say that he had answered that question before the committee and was under no obligation to repeat it publicly and run the risk of a suit, Mr. Chambers answered, "Mr. Hiss was a Communist and may still be."

One week, two weeks, three weeks passed and Mr. Hiss still had not filed suit. Finally, an editorial appeared in the *Washington Post*, a newspaper which had been very favorable to Mr. Hiss editorially and extremely critical of the committee for conducting any hearings at all on the Chambers' charges. But this editorial took Mr. Hiss to task and said that in view of the fact that he had dared Mr. Chambers to make his charge publicly, and he had proceeded to do so, it was now up to him to bring the suit, lest the implication be left that there might be some truth in what Mr. Chambers had said. Finally the suit was brought and a chain reaction was started which was to crack the case wide open.

On November 17, 1948, Mr. Hiss' attorneys took Mr. Chambers' deposition in Baltimore, and in that deposition Mr. Hiss' attorneys were to make their greatest mistake.

They asked Mr. Chambers to produce any documentary evidence that he might have which would establish that Mr. Hiss and he were Communists together. Mr. Chambers produced a thick envelope containing four pages in Mr. Hiss' handwriting and a great number of typewritten documents which he said had been typed on Hiss' typewriter. These documents contained excerpts and summaries of scores of confidential and secret State Department messages.

Now, mark this date, because it is extremely important. This was November 17. That very same day, Mr. Alexander Campbell, the Assistant Attorney General in charge of the Criminal Division, was called by counsel for both sides to come to Baltimore to pick up the documents. Two weeks later on the 1st day of December, a very interesting United Press dispatch appeared in the *Washington Daily News*. This article said in effect that the Justice Department was going to drop the Hiss-Chambers case for lack of evidence and that unless some new evidence was presented the Department would not be able to determine which man was lying.

Now, understand, the dispatch quoted Justice Department sources. And the Department at that time had had in its possession for 2 weeks what Mr. Murphy, the prosecutor in the Hiss trial, has so well called the immutable proof of espionage; page after page after page of confidential, secret State Department documents, some in the handwriting of Mr. Hiss, and others typed on his typewriter. Yet the article said the Justice Department was going to drop the case for lack of evidence.

It was at this point that the Committee on Un-American Activities came back into the picture. Mr. Stripling and I went to Westminster, Md. We questioned Mr. Chambers; we asked him if it were possible that he might have some additional evidence which might bear upon this case in view of the fact that the Justice Department was going to drop it. He was shocked when he learned of this proposed action. He told us that he had been told not to talk about what had happened at the deposition hearing in Baltimore on November 17, but we were able to gather from the conversation with him that some new development in the case had occurred on that date, so when we returned to Washington, D.C., I ordered that a subpena be served upon Mr. Chambers for any other documents that he might have.

As a result of that subpena being served upon him, we obtained the so-called pumpkin papers, 5 rolls of microfilm, containing photostatic copies of literally scores of confidential and secret documents from the State Department and the Bureau of Standards. With this evidence in our possession, we were able to force the matter into the open by convincing the Justice Department that unless it did proceed with its investigation the Committee on Un-American Activities would have to conduct its own investigation of the case.

The rest, of course, is history. Mr. Hiss was indicted on December 15, 1948. The first trial ended in a hung jury, eight for conviction and four for acquittal. Then came the second trial and the guilty verdict reached last Saturday, in which the jurors found Mr. Hiss guilty of perjury in denying that he had turned over these confidential Government documents to Mr. Chambers.

In relating the facts of this case, it has not been my purpose to attempt to convince you that the verdict against Mr. Hiss was justified. There has been too much of a tendency to look upon this case as simply a dramatic conflict between two striking and powerful personalities, Mr. Hiss on the one side and Mr. Chambers on the other.

Whether Mr. Hiss was to be found guilty of the technical crime of perjury with which he was charged was not primarily important as far as the security of the Nation is concerned. What is important is that we not allow the conflict between these two men to obscure the broader implications of the case. This is not a simple case of petty larceny where a common thief sold documents to the highest bidder. This is a case involving far-reaching implications going to the very security of our country, and it is essential that each and every American citizen recognize those implications for what they are.

In the first place, the conspiracy which existed was amazingly effective. Chambers turned over to the Committee and the Justice Department hundreds of pages of confidential and secret documents from the State Department and other Government agencies. The theft of documents in this quantity would in itself be sufficient to cause us grave concern. But Chambers testified that on at least 70 different occasions the members of his espionage ring had obtained a similar amount of documents for transmittal to Soviet agents.

Some State Department apologists have attempted to belittle the gravity of the crime on the ground that the documents were not important. An indication of their importance is that today, 10 years after they were taken from the State Department, three of them have still not been made public because the State Department claims that to make them public would be injurious to the national security of this country.

Even more pertinent on the matter of the importance of the documents is the testimony of Mr. Peurifoy, Assistant Secretary of State in charge of Security, and Mr. Sumner Welles. Both testified that a foreign agent having in possession even one of the many documents which Chambers turned over to the Government could have broken our secret code. This meant, in other words, that the foreign agents who obtained these documents from Chambers broke the American code and were reading all of our confidential communications with foreign governments during that critical period immediately preceding the Hitler-Stalin pact.

The second point we should not forget is that a great number of people other than Mr. Hiss were named by Chambers as being members of his espionage ring. A run-down of the various positions held by the members of the ring indicates the effectiveness with which the conspiracy was able to infiltrate into vital positions, both in Government and in industry. Mr. Chambers' contacts included: Four in the State Department; two in the Treasury Department; two in the Bureau of Standards; one in the Aberdeen Arsenal; a man who later became general counsel of the CIO; one in the Picatinny Arsenal; two in the Electric Boat Co.; one in the Remington Rand Co.; and one in the Illinois Steel Co.

It is significant that the individuals named, almost without exception, held positions of influence where they had access to confidential and secret information. The tragedy of the case is that the great majority of them were American citizens, were graduates of the best colleges and universities in this country, and had yet willingly become members of an organization dedicated to the overthrow of this Government.

At this point I should like to bring to the attention of the Members of the House some facts which have been published in the papers but which have not received the attention they should. Some people still have the idea that all we have in this case is Mr. Chambers' word against Mr. Hiss', and the documentary evidence. But, you will recall that in the first and second trials, another member of the ring, who was a State Department employee, confessed, as Mr. Chambers has confessed. His name is Julian Wadleigh. You may have read his confession which appeared in serial form in the *Washington Post*. Mr. Wadleigh admitted that for a period of over a year, approximately every 2 weeks, he walked out of his State Department office with a brief case full of confidential and secret State Department documents. He would meet Mr. Chambers or the other agent who had been assigned to him at the time on a street corner and he would hand him the brief case.

That night the documents would be microfilmed, and the following morning he would meet him at another rendezvous point, pick up the brief case, take it back to the office, and put the documents in the files so that they would not be missed. Mr. Wadleigh's admission was important primarily because it had the effect of taking the case out of the realm of fantasy and provided solid corroborative evidence to back Chambers' story.

Among the other individuals that Mr. Chambers testified were members of his Communist apparatus was Harry Dexter White, former Assistant Secretary of the Treasury. You will recall that shortly after Mr. White's appearance before the Committee on Un-American Activities in 1943, he passed away. Immediately the critics of the investigations charged that the Committee on Un-American Activities was responsible for his death because we had given credence to the completely unfounded and, note this, undocumented charges that had been made against him by Whittaker Chamber and Elizabeth Bentley. In fact, even today, a member of the faculty of a great New England college is delivering a series of lectures in which he is taking the committee to task for ever conducting any investigation into Mr. White's loyalty.

When Mr. Chambers testified before the committee, in 1948, he stated that Mr. White was not a member of the Communist Party but that he was ideologically in sympathy with the party's objectives. In the second trial, which has just been concluded in New York, Mr. Chambers was questioned further about Mr. White and declared in open court that Mr. White was a source of information for the Soviet espionage ring and that he, Chambers, had received various documents from

White which he turned over to Soviet espionage agents.

Since December of 1948, I have had in my possession photostatic copies of eight pages of documents in the handwriting of Mr. White which Mr. Chambers turned over to the Justice Department on November 17, 1948. I had intended to say nothing about these documents, but since Mr. Chambers testified that he did receive documents from Mr. White, I think the public is entitled to see and consider the evidence.

These facts have definitely been established:

First. A Government handwriting expert, Mr. Harold Gesell of the Veterans' Administration, has established that the documents were in Mr. White's handwriting.

Second. Mr. Chambers, a confessed espionage agent, had the documents in his possession.

Third. A substantial portion of the information contained in these documents were of a confidential nature.

I have the photostats here on the rostrum. Any of you who would like to examine them upon the adjournment of the House today is welcome to do so.

Let me read just one excerpt from this document which may be of interest to you:

"We have agreed to purchase 50,000,000 more ounces of silver from China. China will have left (almost all in London) about 100,000,000 ounces of silver. Her dollar balances are almost all gone."

I discussed this excerpt with a man whose judgment I value in analyzing such documents, and he informed me that that information in the hands of individuals who desired to embarrass the Chinese Government would be almost invaluable.

Then to give you an indication of the scope of the matters covered, let me read just one sentence which appears at the bottom of one of the pages:

"Secretary reading *Red Star Over China* and is quite interested."

The Secretary of the Treasury then, of course, was Mr. Morgenthau. . . .

The third point we should bear in mind is that the conspiracy was so effective, so well-entrenched and so well-defended by apologists in high places that it was not discovered and apprehended until it was too late to prosecute those who were involved in it for the crimes they had committed. There were several occasions during the past 10 years on which, if vigorous action had been taken, the conspiracy could have been exposed and its effectiveness destroyed.

The tragedy of this case is summed up right in the charge itself, because what was this man charged with? With stealing documents? With passing them to a foreign agent? No. He was charged with perjury, for lying when he said that he did not turn over these documents. The reason is that neither Mr. Hiss nor Mr. Wadleigh nor any of the people who were engaged in this activity and who turned over documents, even if they were to admit it today, can be prosecuted under the laws of the land, because the 3-year statute of limitations has lapsed and it is too late to do anything about the crime they have committed.

How did such a situation develop? Let us look at the facts and the record.

Three days after the Hitler-Stalin pact, Mr. Chambers in the company of Mr. Isaac Don Levine went to A.A. Berle, then Assistant Secretary of State in charge of security, and laid the facts concerning the conspiracy before him. He told Mr. Berle, in fact, considerably more about the individuals involved than he told the Committee on Un-American Activities in his first appearance before us on August 3, 1948.

What was done? Mr. Berle says that he checked with Dean Acheson and Felix Frankfurter on the charges concerning the Hiss brothers. I quote from the answer he received from Acheson as Mr. Berle related the conversation to the committee:

"Acheson said he had known the family of these boys from childhood and could vouch for them absolutely. I further found that Mr. Justice Frankfurter would give them exactly similar endorsement. You have therefore a chain of endorsements from the men for whom they had worked."

In any event, the net result was that Chambers returned to New York and never heard from Berle or any other Government official concerning the charges he had made until 1943.

What had been done by Mr. Berle or anybody else in authority to establish the truth or falsity of the very serious charges which Chambers had made? Did he question Hiss? Did he question Chambers? Did he confront the two? The only people who can tell us what was done are the high officials in the Government who were aware of the charges. We do know, in any event, that as far as the individuals named by Chambers were concerned, the only thing that was done to them was to promote each one of them eventually to higher positions of power and influence within the Government.

The failure of the administration to act at that time has been justified in some quarters on the ground that only recently have the people of this country become fully aware of the nature and seriousness of the Communist threat and that it is not fair to use hindsight in criticizing the actions of people in years past when the Communist threat was not recognized as it is today. This argument has some justification, insofar as the period of the war is involved. But it is significant to note that at the time Chambers made his charges to Mr. Berle, the Soviet Union was an ally of Hitler Germany, and in effect, therefore, an enemy along with Germany of all the free peoples of the world including the people of the United States, and the President of the United States, Mr. Roosevelt, so characterized it. There therefore was no excuse whatever for failure at least to investigate the Chambers' charges and to see that the individuals named were "quarantined" so that they would not be in a position to furnish information to a potential enemy of this Nation. In that connection, it is significant to note that information furnished to the Soviet Union during the Hitler-Stalin pact might well have been transmitted by the Russians to their Nazi allies.

In 1943, representatives of the FBI visited Chambers at his farm in Westminster, Md., and he told the story in detail again to them after he had called Mr. Berle and received permission to do so. It can be assumed that this information was made available to officials of the Justice Department and to whatever other agencies whose personnel were directly involved in that they had been named by Chambers as members of his apparatus. Again, however, no action was taken by our officials to establish the truth or falsity of the Chambers charges.

Let me say at this point that I am not critical of the administration or of the officials who were involved for failing to prove that the Chambers charges were true, but I am critical of their failure to investigate those charges or at least to go so far as to bring the two principal characters in the story together as the Committee on Un-American Activities eventually did.

It was after 1943, that Mr. Hiss was Secretary of the Bretton Woods Conference, went to Yalta with President Roosevelt, and acted as Secretary of the UN Conference at San Francisco. It is inconceivable that those who were responsible for appointing him to these high positions, where he had the opportunity to do untold damage to his country by transmitting confidential information to the Soviet Government which they could use in their negotiations with us, were not aware of the charges which had been made.

It will be claimed that at this time we were allies of the Soviet Union and had no reason to suspect that they would engage in espionage against us. But let me say at this point that there is no question whatever but that the top officials of our Government were aware of the fact that the Russians were engaging in espionage activities against us even while they were our allies. The testimony of General Groves before the Committee on Un-American Activities in 1948 on that point is significant. I quote the testimony:

"MR. STRIPLING. General Groves, did you ever report the efforts of the Russian agents to obtain information regarding atomic developments to the President of the United States.

"GENERAL GROVES. Yes.

"MR. STRIPLING. When was that?

"GENERAL GROVES. It would have to be in 1944. It was contained in a report to the President which President Roosevelt read in my presence and the matter was discussed with me. This was just before he left for Yalta. It was brought to the attention of President Truman in the first report that was made to President Truman after he took office, which was as soon after his taking office as the Secretary of War could make an appointment, and on that occasion the written memorandum was read by Mr. Truman."

In other words, concrete information concerning Communist espionage activities in this country was in the hands of both President Roosevelt and President Truman and still no action was taken to check Chambers' charges against officials who held high positions in the Government at that time. . . .

You will note that on several occasions I have pointed out that many of those who were named as being members of espionage rings, when they came before the committee or before the grand jury and were asked about their activities answered by saying, "I refuse to answer the question on the ground that any answer I give to the question might tend to incriminate me." Let me say on that point I do not see how a no answer—"No"—to a question as to whether a person engaged in espionage activities could incriminate anybody. . . .

Shortly before the first trial of Mr. Hiss, I learned that a secret memorandum, dated November 25, 1945, dealing with Soviet espionage in the United States and prepared by an intelligence agency of this Government, was circulated among several key Government departments and was made available to the President. I said nothing at that time about the information which was contained in the memorandum because I did not want to take action which might influence the trial one way or the other. Now that the trial is over, I believe that the country is entitled to the information.

I quote directly from that memorandum:

"Igor Guzenko, former code clerk in the office of Col. Nicholi Zabotin, Soviet military attaché, Ottawa, Canada, when interviewed by a representative of this Bureau and officers of the Royal Canadian Mounted Police, stated that he had been informed by Lieutenant Kulakov in the office of the Soviet military attaché that the Soviets had an agent in the United States in May 1945 who was an assistant to the then Secretary of State, Edward R. Stettinius."

Note the date of this memorandum. Note the position held by the individual alleged to be the Soviet espionage agent—assistant to the Secretary of State, Mr. Stettinius. Mr. Hiss was an assistant to Mr. Stettinius at the Yalta Conference in February of 1945.

I have here Mr. Stettinius' book, *Roosevelt and the Russians*. If you read the book you will find eight different references to Mr. Hiss.

On page 36 it appears that Stettinius reviewed with Hiss and others the following:

First. Establishment of a European high commission.

Second. Treatment of Germany.

Third. The Polish question.

Fourth. Relation between UNRRA and the Soviets.

Fifth. Rights of Americans on control commission of Bulgaria, Rumania and Hungary.

Sixth. Iran.

Seventh. China.

Eighth. Turkish Straits question.

Ninth. International trusteeship.

Page 49: Stettinius had a discussion with Hiss and others on the political and economic situation in Italy.

Pages 83 and 84: Stettinius met Hiss and others "to review our proposals for the conference agenda."

Page 103: Hiss is mentioned as sitting behind the President at the Yalta Conference.

Page 137: Stettinius and Hiss met to "go over notes for the afternoon meeting of the three leaders."

Page 138: At the above meeting, Hiss was sitting behind the President.

Page 195 and 196: Alger Hiss is mentioned as a member of a subcommittee which included Gromyko, which was at work preparing a report.

Page 238: Stettinius "asked Hiss to do a quick summary of the State Department memorandum on the trusteeship."

I will not read further; I think the facts speak for themselves.

Note the source of the information which I have quoted from the memorandum. This is not idle back-fence gossip; this information came straight from a representative of the Soviet Government itself. There is one thing that I have learned in my service on the Committee on Un-American Activities, and that is that the Communists will lie about almost everything but they do not lie to each other about the members of the espionage and underground organizations of which they themselves are members.

They know who their people are.

What was done when this shocking information came to the attention of the officials of our State Department, and the President of the United States? You would think now that Mr. Hiss would be confronted with Mr. Chambers and that the mystery would be cleared up, but instead Mr. Hiss continued to serve in high positions in the State Department until he resigned in January 1947 to take a position as head of the Carnegie Foundation for International Peace. In that connection it is significant to note that when trustees of the Carnegie Foundation questioned Mr. Hiss' former associates in the State Department as to his suitability for that position, he received completely unqualified recommendations from all sides. There was no hint whatever that any question had been raised concerning his loyalty to this nation.

To complete this story of inexcusable inaction upon the part of administration officials to attack and destroy this conspiracy, let me review briefly the conduct of the President and the Department of Justice during the investigation of the case by the Committee on Un-American Activities. On August 5, the day Mr. Hiss first appeared before the committee and denied the charges which had been made against him, the President threw the great power and prestige of his office against the investigation by the committee and for Mr. Hiss by declaring that the hearings of the committee were simply a "red herring."

In other words the "red herring" statement was made in direct reference to the Alger Hiss case.

That same day, he issued a Presidential directive which ordered all administrative agencies of the Government to refuse to turn over any information relating to the loyalty of any Government employee to a congressional committee. This meant that the committee had to conduct its investigation with no assistance whatever from the administrative branch of the Government. Included in this order was, of course, the FBI, who by reason of that fact, was unable to lend assistance to the committee.

The most flagrant action, however, was yet to come. As I have already stated, the day Mr. Chambers turned over documentary evidence in the handwriting of Mr. Hiss, together with typewritten documents which were later established to be written on his typewriter, the Justice Department was immediately notified and the material was on that day, November 17, turned over to Alexander Campbell, head of the Criminal Division of that Department. The various participants in the deposition were directed in the interests of national security to keep silent on the whole matter. I have before me the previously mentioned United Press dispatch which appeared on December 1 in the *Washington Daily News*. Let me read from it directly:

"HISS AND CHAMBERS PERJURY PROBE HITS DEAD END

"The Justice Department is about ready to drop its investigation of the celebrated Alger Hiss–Whittaker Chambers controversy, it was learned today.

"Department officials still have under study the question of a possible perjury prosecution. But officials said privately that unless additional evidence is forthcoming, they are inclined to forget the whole thing.

"One Department source said that on the basis of available evidence, officials in charge of the case believe it would be unwise to take it before a grand jury."

What happened during that critical 2-week period between November 17 when the papers were turned over to the Justice Department and December 1 when this article appeared?

I have learned from personal investigation that no agents of the Department of Justice even approached Mr. Chambers during that period let alone questioned him about the highly important evidence which he had turned over to the Justice Department. In view of the story which appeared on December 1, stating that the Justice Department was ready to drop the investigation for lack of new evidence, the only conclusion which can be drawn when this fact is coupled with the Department's failure to conduct an investigation during that 2-week period is that it was the intention of that Department not to make an investigation unless they were forced to do so.

As a result of having in its possession the microfilm documents, which we obtained on December 2, the committee was able to force the Department to institute an investigation and the result was the eventual indictment of Mr. Hiss by the Federal grand jury. It is significant to note that even as late as December 5, members of the committee learned from an unimpeachable source that Justice Department officials before proceeding with further investigation of Mr. Hiss were considering the possibility of indicting Mr. Chambers for technical perjury due to his failure to tell the whole story when he first appeared before the committee and the grand jury. For that reason, I publicly stated on that same day that if the Department should proceed in that manner, it would in effect mean that Mr. Hiss and the others named by Mr. Chambers as being members of an espionage group could not possibly be proceeded against due to the fact that the principal witness against them would be an indicted perjurer. . . .

The President had referred to the case as a "red herring" and did so even after the indictment. The Secretary of State, Mr. Acheson, before his confirmation, declared his friendship for Mr. Hiss and the implication of his declaration was that he had faith in his innocence. Two justices of the Supreme Court, Mr. Frankfurter and Mr. Reed, in an unprecedented action, appeared as character witnesses for Mr. Hiss. Judge Kaufman, who presided at the trial, stepped off the bench and shook hands with these defense witnesses, one of many of his actions during the trial in which he showed his obvious bias for the defendant. The wife of the former President of the United States, Mrs. Roosevelt, on several occasions during the two trials, publicly defended Mr. Hiss in her news columns. Among the high Government officials who testified in his behalf were Mr. Philip Jessup, then President Truman's ambassador at large in Europe, and now the architect of our far-eastern policy; the Governor of Illinois, Mr. Stevenson; Judge Wyzski, of the United States District Court, Boston; and Francis B. Sayre, Assistant Secretary of State.

I have mentioned the individuals who have come to Mr. Hiss' defense, because this is an outstanding example of how effectively the conspiracy was concealed and how far it was able to reach into high places in our Government to obtain apologists for its members.

Why was it that administration officials persisted in their refusal to act through the years, even when substantial evidence of espionage activities was brought to their attention? A number of reasons have been suggested for this failure.

It has been said that the Soviet Union was an ally of the United States and that therefore we should take a charitable attitude toward those administration officials who failed to act when the evidence was presented to them. But Mr. Chambers first presented his information to Mr. Berle during the period of the Hitler-Stalin pact when it could not be said, under any stretch of the imagination, that the Soviet Union was an ally of this country. Nor can anyone possibly justify the obstructive policies followed by administration leaders even as late as 1943 when the Committee on Un-American Activities was attempting to bring all the facts out into the open and when our announced national policy was to contain communism abroad if not at home.

On the other extreme, there are some who claim that administration officials failed to act because they were Communist or pro-Communist. I do not accept this charge as a fair one as applied at least to the great majority of those officials who could and should have acted on the evidence which was laid before them through the years.

The reason for their failure to act was not that they were disloyal, but this in my opinion makes that failure even more inexcusable.

What was happening was that the administration leaders were treating the reports of Communist espionage on a "politics-as-usual" basis. It is customary practice for any administration, be it Republican or Democrat, to resist the disclosure of facts which might be embarrassing to that administration in an election. This is a statement of fact though, of course, I do not mean to justify that practice, regardless of the nature of the skeleton in the political closet.

Because they treated Communist infiltration into our American institutions like any ordinary petty political scandal, the administration officials responsible for this failure to act against the Communist conspiracy rendered the greatest possible disservice to the people of the Nation.

It is essential that we learn the tragic lessons which the Hiss case has so vividly portrayed, and develop a policy which will reduce the possibility for the existence and successful operation of such a conspiracy in the future. I have some recommendations to make along those lines, most of which are not new, but which I reiterate because I feel that they are essential to our national security.

First. Above all, we must give complete and unqualified support to the FBI, and to J. Edgar Hoover, its chief. Mr. Hoover recognized the Communist threat long before other top officials recognized its existence. The FBI in this trial did an amazingly effective job of running down trails over 10 years old and in developing evidence which made the prosecution successful.

I note in the papers this morning that the National Lawyers Guild has again launched an all-out attack against the FBI. The character of the guild is well illustrated by the fact that 5 of the lawyers for the 11 convicted Communists in New York City, who were cited by Judge Medina for contempt of court because of their disgraceful conduct, are prominent members of the Lawyers Guild. Let me just say this: That when the National Lawyers Guild or any similar organization is successful in obtaining an investigation of the FBI and access to its records, a fatal blow will have been struck against the protective security forces of this Nation. I am sure that the Members of the House will join with me in resisting such an attack and in supporting the finest police organization which exists in a free Nation today. [Applause.]

Second. Time will not permit me to discuss all the steps which should be taken in the field of legislation if we are adequately to control and expose the Communist conspiracy in this country. but the very least that should be done during this session of Congress is to extend the statute of limitations on espionage cases from 3 to 10 years. The fact that an espionage agent is able to conceal his activities so effectively that he is not apprehended until after the statutory period has elapsed makes the crime even more infamous and serious in nature. Our present laws are totally inadequate to deal with the new types of espionage which have been developed so effectively by the Communists.

Third. The Committee on Un-American Activities should receive the whole-hearted support of the House. It is well recognized that had the committee not been in existence, the Hiss conspiracy might never have been exposed.

Let me say at this point that I know the Members of this House are aware of the fact that membership on the Committee on Un-American Activities should not be sought by any person who desires to avoid probably the most unpleasant and thankless assignment in the Congress. I trust that

Members from both sides will join together in supporting that committee and its members in the years to come, and in seeing to it that it gets the authority and the funds to conduct honest, intelligent, and fair investigations of Communists and other subversive groups in this country.

Fourth. It is necessary that we completely overhaul our system of checking the loyalty of Federal employees. Mr. Hiss would have passed the present loyalty tests with flying colors. The loyalty checks are based primarily on open affiliations with Communist-front organizations. Underground Communists and espionage agents have no open affiliations and it is therefore almost impossible to apprehend them through a routine loyalty investigation under the President's order. Serious consideration should be given to changing the entire approach under the loyalty order and placing the program on a security risk rather than loyalty basis. In this way, where there is any doubt about an individual who has access to confidential information, that doubt can be resolved in favor of the Government without the necessity of proving disloyalty and thereby reflecting on the character of a possibly loyal but indiscreet Government employee.

Fifth. Most important of all, we must develop and put into effect an extensive educational program which will teach the American people the truth about Communism as well as the truth about democracy. The tragedy of this case is that men like Alger Hiss who come from good families, are graduates of our best schools, and are awarded the highest honors in Government service, find the Communist ideology more attractive than American democracy.

This is a serious reflection on our educational system, and it is essential that we remedy the situation if we are to survive as a free people. The statement of Mr. John Foster Dulles when he commented upon the Hiss verdict last Saturday is particularly pertinent:

"The conviction of Alger Hiss is human tragedy. It is tragic that so great promise should have come to so inglorious an end. But the greater tragedy is that seemingly our national ideals no longer inspire the loyal devotion needed for their defense."

Five years ago, at the time of the Dumbarton Oaks Conference in 1944, when Alger Hiss served as director of our secretariat, the number of people in the world in the Soviet orbit was 180,000,000, approximately the population of the Soviet Union. Today there are 800,000,000 in the world under the domination of Soviet totalitarianism. On our side we have 540,000,000. There are 600,000,000 residents of United Nations countries which are classified as neutral, such as India, Pakistan, and Sweden. In other words, in 1944, before Dumbarton Oaks, Teheran, Yalta, and Potsdam, the odds were 9 to 1 in our favor. Today, since those conferences, the odds are 5 to 3 against us.

The great lesson which should be learned from the Alger Hiss case is that we are not just dealing with espionage agents who get 30 pieces of silver to obtain the blueprint of a new weapon—the Communists do that, too—but this is a far more sinister type of activity, because it permits the enemy to guide and shape our policy; it disarms and dooms our diplomats to defeat in advance before they go to conferences; traitors in the high councils of our own Government make sure that the deck is stacked on the Soviet side of the diplomatic table. America today stands almost alone between Communism and the free nations of the world. We owe a solemn duty, not only to our own people but to free peoples everywhere on both sides of the iron curtain, to expose this sinister conspiracy for what it is, to roll back the Red tide which to date has swept everything before it, and to prove to peoples everywhere that the hope for the world lies not in turning toward totalitarian dictatorship but in developing a strong, free, and intelligent democracy.

6.

The "Pink Sheet" (1950)

Printed on pink paper, this flier from Nixon's 1950 Senate run became an enduring symbol of his slashing campaign style. Critics later pointed out of its central claim—that his opponent Helen Gahagan Douglas "voted the same as Marcantonio 354 times"—that Nixon had voted the same as the left-wing Bronx congressman Vito Marcantonio a couple of hundred times himself.

Douglas-Marcantonio Voting Record

Many persons have requested a comparison of the voting records of Congresswoman Helen Douglas and the notorious Communist party-liner, Congress Vito Marantonio of New York.

Mrs. Douglas and Marcantonio have been members of Congress together since January 1, 1945. During that period, Mrs. Douglas voted the same as Marcantonio 354 times. While it should not be expected that a member of the House of Representatives should always vote in opposition to Marcantonio, it is significant to note, not only the great number of times which Mrs. Douglas voted in agreement with him, but also the issues on which almost without exception they always saw eye to eye, to-wit: Un-American Activities and Internal Security.

Here is the Record!

Votes against Committee On Un-American Activities

Both Douglas and Marcantonio voted against establishing the Committee on Un-American Activities. 1/3/45. Bill passed.

Both voted on three separate occasions against contempt proceedings against persons and organizations which refused to reveal records or answer whether they were Communists. 4/16/46, 6/26/46, 11/24/47. Bills passed.

Both voted on four separate occasions against allowing funds for investigation by the Un-American Activities Committee. 3/17/46, 3/9/48, 2/9/49, 3/23/50. (The last vote was 348 to 12.) All bills passed.

Communist-Line Foreign Policy Votes

Both voted against Greek-

Votes against Loyalty and Security Legislation

Both voted on two separate occasions against bills requiring loyalty checks for Federal employees. 7/15/47, 6/29/49. Bills passed.

Both voted against the Subversive Activities Control Act of 1948, requiring registration with the Attorney General of Communist party members and communist controlled organizations. Bill passed, 319 to 58. 5/19/48.

AND AFTER KOREA both again voted against it. Bill passed 8/29/50, 354 to 20.

AFTER KOREA, on July 12, 1950, Marcantonio and Douglas and 12 others voted against the Security Bill, to permit the heads of key National Defense departments, such as the Atomic Energy Commission, to discharge government workers found to be

Turkish Aid Bill. 5/9/47. (It has been established that without this aid Greece and Turkey would have gone behind the Iron Curtain.) Bill passed.

Both voted on two occasions against free press amendment to [United Nations Relief and Rehabilitation Administration] appropriation bill, providing that no funds should be furnished to any country which refused to allow free access to the news of activities of the UNRRA by press and radio representatives of the United States. 11/1/45, 6/28/46. Bills passed. (This would in effect have denied American relief funds to Communist dominated countries.)

Both voted against refusing Foreign Relief to Soviet-dominated countries UNLESS supervised by Americans. 4/30/47. Bill passed 324 to 75.

Vote against National Defense

Both voted against the Selective Service Act of 1948. 6/18/48. Bill passed.

poor security risks! Bill passed, 327 to 14.

Vote against California

Both recorded against confirming title to Tidelands in California and the other states affected. 4/30/48. Bill passed 257-29.

Votes against Congressional Investigation of Communist and Other Illegal Activities

Both voted against investigating the "whitewash" of the AMERASIA case. 4/18/46. Bill passed.

Both voted against investigating why the Soviet Union was buying as many as 60,000 United States patents at one time. 3/4/47. Bill passed.

Both voted against continuing investigation of numerous instances of illegal action by OPA and the War Labor Board. 1/18/45. Bill passed.

Both voted on two occasions against allowing Congress to have access to government records necessary to the conduct of investigations by Senate and House Committees. 4/22/48. 5/13/48. Bills passed.

ON ALL OF THE ABOVE VOTES which have occurred since Congressman Nixon took office on January 1, 1947, HE has voted exactly opposite to the Douglas-Marcantonio Axis!

After studying the voting comparison between Mrs. Douglas and Marcantonio, is it any wonder that the Communist line newspaper, the Daily People's World, in its lead editorial on January 31, 1950, labeled Congressman Nixon as "The Man To Beat" in this Senate race and that the Communist newspaper, the New York Daily Worker, in the issue of July 28, 1947, selected Mrs. Douglas with Marcantonio as "One of the Heroes of the 80th Congress."

REMEMBER! The United States Senate votes on ratifying international treaties and confirming presidential appointments. Would California send Marcantonio to the United States Senate?

7.

The "Checkers Speech" (September 23, 1952)

Nixon's most famous early speech was a masterpiece of his key political method: when in trouble, reframe your accusers as the offending party and yourself as the victim. Here, the Republican vice presidential nominee stood accused of a specific charge: that he had benefited from an improper campaign fund. Brilliantly, he twisted it into something entirely different, and more easily debunked: that he had exploited his office to make himself rich. His cynically sentimental performance—he was just another ordinary middle-class striver; the fund was a boon to the public interest, not a bane—included several narratively convenient falsehoods (for instance, the little dog Checkers, which he deviously implied his villainous enemies were attempting to take from his family, was not named by his six-year-old daughter, but came to them already named). It also included a clever low blow that the record-high television audience wouldn't have noted: a hint to presidential nominee Dwight D. Eisenhower that he knew of financial improprieties in his own past ("a man that's to be President . . . must have the confidence of all the people"), and that if Eisenhower didn't play ball he'd lower the boom on him. He also offered a thin defense Nixon loyalists would have occasion to repeat a dozen years later: everyone does it.

But it was also a remarkably courageous act. Eisenhower's handlers had put Nixon on live television broadcast in order for him to deliver his resignation speech. Instead, he displayed before the world his most admirable quality: a refusal to back down before intimidation. The Republican Party was inundated with more than two million telegrams demanding that he be kept on the ticket. The nation's opinion elite, meanwhile, considered the broadcast an embarrassing farce; the whole business cemented Nixon's investiture as American liberalism's preeminent bête noire.

My Fellow Americans,
I come before you tonight as a candidate for the Vice Presidency and as a man whose honesty and integrity has been questioned.

Now, the usual political thing to do when charges are made against you is to either ignore them or to deny them without giving details. I believe we've had enough of that in the United States, particularly with the present Administration in Washington, D.C. To me the office of the Vice Presidency of the United States is a great office, and I feel that the people have got to have confidence in the integrity of the men who run for that office and who might obtain it.

I have a theory, too, that the best and only answer to a smear or to an honest misunderstanding of the facts is to tell the truth. And that's why I'm here tonight. I want to tell you my side of the case. I'm sure that you have read the charge, and you've heard it, that I, Senator Nixon, took $18,000 from a group of my supporters.

Now, was that wrong? And let me say that it was wrong. I'm saying, incidentally, that it was wrong, not just illegal, because it isn't a question of whether it was legal or illegal, that isn't enough. The question is, was it morally wrong? I say that it was morally wrong—if any of that $18,000 went to Senator Nixon, for my personal use. I say that it was morally wrong if it was secretly given and secretly handled. And I say that it was morally wrong if any of the contributors got special favors for the contributions that they made.

And now to answer those questions let me say this: Not one cent of the $18,000 or any other money of that type ever went to me for my personal use. Every penny of it was used to pay for political expenses that I did not think should be charged to the taxpayers of the United States. It was not a secret fund. As a matter of fact, when I was on "Meet the Press"—some of you may have seen it last Sunday—Peter Edson came up to me after the program, and he said, "Dick, what about this 'fund' we hear about?" And I said, "Well, there's no secret about it. Go out and see Dana Smith who was the administrator of the fund."

And I gave him his address. And I said you will find that the purpose of the fund simply was to defray political expenses that I did not feel should be charged to the Government.

And third, let me point out—and I want to make this particularly clear—that no contributor to this fund, no contributor to any of my campaigns, has ever received any consideration that he would not have received as an ordinary constituent. I just don't believe in that, and I can say that never, while I have been in the Senate of the United States, as far as the people that contributed to this fund are concerned, have I made a telephone call for them to an agency, or have I gone down to an agency in their behalf. And the records will show that, the records which are in the hands of the administration.

Well, then, some of you will say, and rightly, "Well, what did you use the fund for, Senator?" "Why did you have to have it?" Let me tell you in just a word how a Senate office operates. First of all, a Senator gets 15,000 dollars a year in salary. He gets enough money to pay for one trip a year—a round trip, that is—for himself and his family between his home and Washington, D.C. And then he gets an allowance to handle the people that work in his office to handle his mail. And the allowance for my State of California is enough to hire 13 people. And let me say, incidentally, that

that allowance is not paid to the Senator. It's paid directly to the individuals that the Senator puts on his payroll. But all of these people and all of these allowances are for strictly official business; business, for example, when a constituent writes in and wants you to go down to the Veteran's Administration and get some information about his GI policy—items of that type, for example. But there are other expenses which are not covered by the Government. And I think I can best discuss those expenses by asking you some questions.

Do you think that when I or any other Senator makes a political speech, has it printed, should charge the printing of that speech and the mailing of that speech to the taxpayers? Do you think, for example, when I or any other Senator makes a trip to his home State to make a purely political speech that the cost of that trip should be charged to the taxpayers? Do you think when a Senator makes political broadcasts or political television broadcasts, radio or television, that the expense of those broadcasts should be charged to the taxpayers? Well I know what your answer is. It's the same answer that audiences give me whenever I discuss this particular problem: The answer is no. The taxpayers shouldn't be required to finance items which are not official business but which are primarily political business.

Well, then the question arises, you say, "Well, how do you pay for these and how can you do it legally?" And there are several ways that it can be done, incidentally, and that it is done legally in the United States Senate and in the Congress. The first way is to be a rich man. I don't happen to be a rich man, so I couldn't use that one. Another way that is used is to put your wife on the payroll. Let me say, incidentally, that my opponent, my opposite number for the Vice Presidency on the Democratic ticket, does have his wife on the payroll and has had it—her on his payroll for the ten years—for the past ten years. Now just let me say this: That's his business, and I'm not critical of him for doing that. You will have to pass judgment on that particular point.

But I have never done that for this reason: I have found that there are so many deserving stenographers and secretaries in Washington that needed the work that I just didn't feel it was right to put my wife on the payroll.

My wife's sitting over here. She's a wonderful stenographer. She used to teach stenography and she used to teach shorthand in high school. That was when I met her. And I can tell you folks that she's worked many hours at night and many hours on Saturdays and Sundays in my office, and she's done a fine job, and I am proud to say tonight that in the six years I've been in the House and the Senate of the United States, Pat Nixon has never been on the Government payroll.

What are other ways that these finances can be taken care of? Some who are lawyers, and I happen to be a lawyer, continue to practice law, but I haven't been able to do that. I'm so far away from California that I've been so busy with my senatorial work that I have not engaged in any legal practice. And, also, as far as law practice is concerned, it seemed to me that the relationship between an attorney and the client was so personal that you couldn't possibly represent a man as an attorney and then have an unbiased view when he presented his case to you in the event that he had one before Government.

And so I felt that the best way to handle these necessary political expenses of getting my message to the American people and the speeches I made—the speeches that I had printed for the most part concerned this one message of exposing this Administration, the Communism in it, the corruption in it—the only way that I could do that was to accept the aid which people in my home State of California, who contributed to my campaign and who continued to make these contributions after I was elected, were glad to make.

And let me say I'm proud of the fact that not one of them has ever asked me for a special favor. I'm proud of the fact that not one of them has ever asked me to vote on a bill other than as my own conscience would dictate. And I am proud of the fact that the taxpayers, by subterfuge or otherwise, have never paid one dime for expenses which I thought were political and shouldn't be charged to the taxpayers.

Let me say, incidentally, that some of you may say, "Well, that's all right, Senator, that's your explanation, but have you got any proof?" And I'd like to tell you this evening that just an hour ago we received an independent audit of this entire fund. I suggested to Governor Sherman Adams, who is the Chief of Staff of the Dwight Eisenhower campaign, that an independent audit and legal report be obtained, and I have that audit here in my hands. It's an audit made by the Price Waterhouse & Company firm, and the legal opinion by Gibson, Dunn, & Crutcher, lawyers in Los Angeles, the biggest law firm, and incidentally, one of the best ones in Los Angeles.

I am proud to be able to report to you tonight that this audit and this legal opinion is being forwarded to General Eisenhower. And I'd like to read to you the opinion that was prepared by Gibson, Dunn, & Crutcher, and based on all the pertinent laws and statutes, together with the audit report prepared by the certified public accountants. Quote:

"It is our conclusion that Senator Nixon did not obtain any financial gain from the collection and disbursement of the fund by Dana Smith; that Senator Nixon did not violate any federal or state law by reason of the operation of the fund; and that neither the portion of the fund paid by Dana Smith directly to third persons, nor the portion paid to Senator Nixon, to reimburse him for designated office expenses, constituted income to the Senator which was either reportable or taxable as income under applicable tax laws.

"Gibson, Dunn, & Crutcher,

"by Elmo H. Conley"

Now that, my friends, is not Nixon speaking, but that's an independent audit which was requested, because I want the American people to know all the facts, and I am not afraid of having independent people go in and check the facts, and that is exactly what they did. But then I realized that there are still some who may say, and rightfully so—and let me say that I recognize that some will continue to smear regardless of what the truth may be—but that there has been, understandably, some honest misunderstanding on this matter, and there are some that will say, "Well, maybe you were able, Senator, to fake this thing. How can we believe what you say? After all, is there a possibility that maybe you got some sums in cash? Is there a possibility that you may have feathered your own nest?" And so now, what I am going to do—and incidentally this is unprecedented in the history of American politics—I am going at this time to give to this television and radio audio—audience, a complete financial history, everything I've earned, everything I've spent, everything I own. And I want you to know the facts.

I'll have to start early. I was born in 1913. Our family was one of modest circumstances, and most of my early life was spent in a store out in East Whittier. It was a grocery store, one of those family enterprises. The only reason we were able to make it go was because my mother and dad had five boys, and we all worked in the store. I worked my way through college, and, to a great extent, through law school. And then in 1940, probably the best thing that ever happened to me happened. I married Pat who's sitting over here. We had a rather difficult time after we were married, like so many of the young couples who may be listening to us. I practiced law. She continued to teach school.

Then, in 1942, I went into the service. Let me say that my service record was not a particularly unusual one. I went to the South Pacific. I guess I'm entitled to a couple of battle stars. I got a couple of letters of commendation. But I was just there when the bombs were falling. And then I returned—returned to the United States, and in 1946, I ran for the Congress. When we came out of the war—Pat and I—Pat during the war had worked as a stenographer, and in a bank, and as an economist for a Government agency—and when we came out, the total of our savings, from both my law practice, her teaching and all the time that I was in the war, the total for that entire period was just a little less than 10,000 dollars. Every cent of that, incidentally, was in Government bonds. Well that's where we start, when I go into politics.

Now, what have I earned since I went into politics? Well, here it is. I've jotted it down. Let me read the notes. First of all, I've had my salary as a Congressman and as a Senator. Second, I have received a total in this past six years of $1600 from estates which were in my law firm at the time that I severed my connection with it. And, incidentally, as I said before, I have not engaged in any legal practice and have not accepted any fees from business that came into the firm after I went into politics. I have made an average of approximately $1500 a year from nonpolitical speaking engagements and lectures.

And then, fortunately, we've inherited a little money. Pat sold her interest in her father's estate for $3,000, and I inherited $1500 from my grandfather. We lived rather modestly. For four years we lived in an apartment in Parkfairfax, in Alexandria, Virginia. The rent was $80 a month. And we saved for the time that we could buy a house. Now, that was what we took in. What did we do with this money? What do we have today to show for it? This will surprise you because it is so little, I suppose, as standards generally go of people in public life.

First of all, we've got a house in Washington, which cost $41,000 and on which we owe $20,000. We have a house in Whittier, California which cost $13,000 and on which we owe $3000. My folks are living there at the present time. I have just 4000 dollars in life insurance, plus my GI policy which I've never been able to convert, and which will run out in two years. I have no life insurance whatever on Pat. I have no life insurance on our two youngsters, Tricia and Julie. I own a 1950 Oldsmobile car. We have our furniture. We have no stocks and bonds of any type. We have no interest of any kind, direct or indirect, in any business. Now, that's what we have. What do we owe?

Well in addition to the mortgage, the $20,000 mortgage on the house in Washington, the $10,000 one on the house in Whittier, I owe $4500 to the Riggs Bank in Washington, D.C., with interest 4 and ½ percent. I owe 3500 dollars to my parents, and the interest on that loan, which I pay regularly, because it's the part of the savings they made through the years they were working so hard—I pay regularly 4 percent interest. And then I have a $500 loan, which I have on my life insurance.

Well, that's about it. That's what we have. And that's what we owe. It isn't very much. But Pat and I have the satisfaction that every dime that we've got is honestly ours. I should say this, that

Pat doesn't have a mink coat. But she does have a respectable Republican cloth coat, and I always tell her she'd look good in anything.

One other thing I probably should tell you, because if I don't they'll probably be saying this about me, too. We did get something, a gift, after the election. A man down in Texas heard Pat on the radio mention the fact that our two youngsters would like to have a dog. And believe it or not, the day before we left on this campaign trip we got a message from Union Station in Baltimore, saying they had a package for us. We went down to get it. You know what it was? It was a little cocker spaniel dog in a crate that he'd sent all the way from Texas, black and white, spotted. And our little girl Tricia, the six year old, named it "Checkers." And you know, the kids, like all kids, love the dog, and I just want to say this, right now, that regardless of what they say about it, we're gonna keep it.

It isn't easy to come before a nationwide audience and bare your life, as I've done. But I want to say some things before I conclude that I think most of you will agree on. Mr. Mitchell, the Chairman of the Democratic National Committee, made this statement—that if a man couldn't afford to be in the United States Senate, he shouldn't run for the Senate. And I just want to make my position clear. I don't agree with Mr. Mitchell when he says that only a rich man should serve his Government in the United States Senate or in the Congress. I don't believe that represents the thinking of the Democratic Party, and I know that it doesn't represent the thinking of the Republican Party.

I believe that it's fine that a man like Governor Stevenson, who inherited a fortune from his father, can run for President. But I also feel that it's essential in this country of ours that a man of modest means can also run for President, because, you know, remember Abraham Lincoln, you remember what he said: "God must have loved the common people—he made so many of them."

And now I'm going to suggest some courses of conduct. First of all, you have read in the papers about other funds, now. Mr. Stevenson apparently had a couple—one of them in which a group of business people paid and helped to supplement the salaries of State employees. Here is where the money went directly into their pockets, and I think that what Mr. Stevenson should do should be to come before the American people, as I have, give the names of the people that contributed to that fund, give the names of the people who put this money into their pockets at the same time that they were receiving money from their State government and see what favors, if any, they gave out for that.

I don't condemn Mr. Stevenson for what he did, but until the facts are in there is a doubt that will be raised. And as far as Mr. Sparkman is concerned, I would suggest the same thing. He's had his wife on the payroll. I don't condemn him for that, but I think that he should come before the American people and indicate what outside sources of income he has had. I would suggest that under the circumstances both Mr. Sparkman and Mr. Stevenson should come before the American people, as I have, and make a complete financial statement as to their financial history, and if they don't it will be an admission that they have something to hide. And I think you will agree with me—because, folks, remember, a man that's to be President of the United States, a man that's to be Vice President of the United States, must have the confidence of all the people. And that's why I'm doing what I'm doing. And that's why I suggest that Mr. Stevenson and Mr. Sparkman, since they are under attack, should do what I'm doing.

Now let me say this: I know that this is not the last of the smears. In spite of my explanation tonight, other smears will be made. Others have been made in the past. And the purpose of the smears, I know, is this: to silence me; to make me let up. Well, they just don't know who they're dealing with. I'm going to tell you this: I remember in the dark days of the Hiss case some of the same columnists, some of the same radio commentators who are attacking me now and misrepresenting my position, were violently opposing me at the time I was after Alger Hiss. But I continued to fight because I knew I was right, and I can say to this great television and radio audience that I have no apologies to the American people for my part in putting Alger Hiss where he is today. And as far as this is concerned, I intend to continue to fight. . . .

III. Vice President

8.

"When you go out to shoot rats" (March 13, 1954)

On the campaign trail and in the Eisenhower administration, Nixon's role was to serve as Eisenhower's hatchet man: whenever there had been a dirty job to get done, he had been there to do it—thus preserving Eisenhower's political capital as the nation's warm and wise national grandfather. In 1954, after years of benefiting from Joseph McCarthy's fusillades against Democrats, the Republican establishment judged McCarthy had gone too far with his attacks on the army, and sent Nixon to carry out the hit on TV—a surgical strike designed to both neutralize a political embarrassment, and preserve the notion of the Democrats as a party that coddled Communists.

. . . We know from studying history of the past ten years that men like Alger Hiss and Harry White turned over secret papers to the Communists and we know that also they were in a position to exert influence for the Communists on policies of the United States.

We know that our atomic experts say that the Russians got the secret of the atomic bomb three to five years before they would have gotten it because of the help they received from Communist spies right here in the United States.

And consequently because we recognize the present danger under the President's direction the executive branch of this government has developed a program to deal with the problem.

Now this program does two things. First, we made just as sure as we can that we don't put the Communists on the payroll in the first place and second, under a new security risk program we recognize that it's a privilege, not a right to work for the government, and that we should remove from the payroll those of doubtful loyalty and those who might be easy prey to espionage agents because of their personal habits or their backgrounds.

Now how does this policy work? Well, since May when the policy was announced, thoroughly and effectively under this program we have been weeding out individuals of this type. And to give you an idea, I have here a breakdown of the files of over 2,400 people who have left the federal payrolls either by resignation or discharge under this program since May.

And a great majority of these, incidentally, were inherited from the previous administration.

This is what their files show: 422 of the files showed that they contained information indicating subversive activities or associations; 198 of them showed information indicating sexual perversion; 611 showed information indicating convictions for felonies or misdemeanors and 1,424 of these files showed information indicating untrustworthiness, drunkenness, mental instability or possible exposure to blackmail.

I think that all of you will agree that people with information like that in their files shouldn't be working for the federal government. That's good reasoning and that's why they aren't working for the federal government today.

Now, that's what the administration in the executive branch has done. In addition, the President and this administration recognizes the right and the responsibility of congressional committees to investigate in this field.

But here I want to make a statement that some of you are going to agree with and some of you are not, but it should be made. The President, this administration, the responsible leadership of the Republican Party insists that whether in the executive branch of the government or the legislative branch of the government the procedures for dealing with the threat of Communism in the United States must be fair and they must be proper.

Now I can imagine that some of you who are listening will say, "Well, why all of this hullabaloo about being fair when you're dealing with a gang of traitors?"

As a matter of fact I've heard people say, "After all, they're a bunch of rats. What we ought to do is to go out and shoot 'em." Well, I'll agree that they're a bunch of rats, but just remember this. When you go out to shoot rats, you have to shoot straight, because when you shoot wildly it not only means that the rat may get away more easily, you make it easier on the rat.

But you might hit someone else who's trying to shoot rats too. And so we've got to be fair. For two very good reasons: One, because it's right, and two, because it's the most effective way of doing the job.

Why is it right? Well, why do we fight Communism in the first place? Because Communism threatens freedom and when we use unfair methods for fighting Communists we help destroy freedom ourselves.

Now why is it the most effective way to fight Communism, to do it fairly, I mean? Now may I say that I've had some experience in this field. I think I know what I'm talking about. And I know that even when you do it fairly you will get criticism from some of those who object not to how you are investigating but who object to what you are investigating.

And when you do it unfairly and with irresponsibility all you do is give ammunition to those who oppose any action against the Communists. And when through carelessness you lump the innocent and the guilty together, what you do is to give the guilty a chance to pull the cloak of innocence around themselves.

Now, in recent weeks we've seen a striking example of the truth of these principles I've just enunciated. Men who have in the past done effective work exposing Communists in this country have, by reckless talk and questionable method, made themselves the issue rather than the cause they believe in so deeply.

And when they've done this, you see, they not only have diverted attention from the danger of Communism, diverted from that danger to themselves, but also they have allowed those whose primary objective is to defeat the Eisenhower Administration to divert attention from its great program to these individuals who follow these methods. . . .

9.

The "Kitchen Debate" (July 24, 1959)

The encounter between Vice President Nixon and Soviet Premier Nikita Khrushchev at a Moscow trade fair was a surreal Cold War moment. The intense interest it inspired was partly a function of its novelty. Nixon's visit to the Soviet Union—followed two months later by a visit by Khrushchev to the United States, in which the premier tried and failed to visit Disneyland—marked a rare lull in U.S.-Soviet tensions. Khrushchev was all but mythic as a bogeyman. And here he was, in the flesh, walking and talking, as what was supposed to be an opportunity to show off a new American technology—videotape—broke out into a spirited exchange with Nixon, who handled him with poise and aplomb.

No copy of the original tape exists—which in itself was apparently a brief record of a multiday dialogue—and the existing transcripts are discontinuous and contradictory. But what remains is, among other things, a fascinating record of American consumerist ideology (note Nixon's assertion of color TV as a victory in the Cold War); and a testament to Nixon's evolution away from a public identity as a simplistic hard-line Red hunter.

KHRUSHCHEV: In another seven years, we will be on the same level as America [Russians applaud]. . . .

NIXON: [pointing to American workmen] With men like that we are strong. But these men, Soviet and American, work together well for peace, even as they have worked together in building this exhibition. This is the way it should be. Your remarks are in the tradition of what we have come to expect—sweeping and extemporaneous. Later on we will both have an opportunity to speak and consequently I will not comment on the various points that you raised, except to say this—this color television is one of the most advanced developments in communication that we have. I can only say that if this competition in which you plan to outstrip us is to do the best for both of our people and for peoples everywhere, there must be a free exchange of ideas. After all, you don't know everything.

KHRUSHCHEV: If you don't know everything, you don't know anything about Communism except fear of it.

NIXON: There are some instances where you may be ahead of us, for example, in the development of the thrust of your rockets for the investigation of outer space; there may be some instances in which we are ahead of you—in color television, for instance.

KHRUSHCHEV: No, we are up with you on this, too. We have bested you in one technique and also in the other.

NIXON: You see, you never concede anything.

KHRUSHCHEV: I do not give up.

NIXON: Wait till you see the picture. Let's have far more communication and exchange in this very area that we speak of. We should hear you more on our televisions. You should hear us more on yours.

KHRUSHCHEV: That's a good idea. Let's do it like this. You appear before our people. We will appear before your people. People will see and appreciate this.

NIXON: There is not a day in the United States when we cannot read what you say. When Kozlov was speaking in California about peace, you were talking here in somewhat different terms. This was reported extensively in the American press. Never make a statement here if you don't want it to be read in the United States. I can promise you every word you say will be translated into English.

KHRUSHCHEV: I doubt it. I want you to give your word that this speech of mine will be heard by the American people. [They shake hands]

NIXON: By the same token, everything I say will be translated and heard all over the Soviet Union?

KHRUSHCHEV: That's agreed.

NIXON: You must not be afraid of ideas.

KHRUSHCHEV: We are telling you not to be afraid of ideas. We have no reason to be afraid. We have already broken free from such a situation.

NIXON: Well, then, let's have more exchange of them. We are all agreed on that. All right? All right?

KHRUSHCHEV: Fine. [aside] Agree to what? All right, I am in agreement. But I want to stress what I am in agreement with. I know that I am dealing with a very good lawyer. . . . You are a lawyer for capitalism and I am a lawyer for communism. Let's compare.

NIXON: The way you dominate the conversation you would make a good lawyer yourself. If you were in the United States Senate you would be accused of filibustering. [halting Khrushchev at model kitchen in model house] You had a very nice house in your exhibition in New York. My wife and I saw and enjoyed it very much. I want to show you this kitchen. It is like those of our houses in California.

KHRUSHCHEV: [after Nixon called attention to a built-in panel-controlled washing machine]: We have such things.

NIXON: This is the newest model. This is the kind which is built in thousands of units for direct installation in the houses. In America, we like to make life easier for women. . . .

KHRUSHCHEV: Your capitalistic attitude toward women does not occur under Communism.

NIXON: I think that this attitude toward women is universal. What we want to do is make easier the lives of our housewives. . . . This house can be bought for $14,000, and most American [veterans] can buy a home in the bracket of $10,000 to $15,000. Let me give you an example that you can appreciate. Our steel workers, as you know, are on strike. But any steel worker could buy this house. They earn $3 an hour. This house costs about $100 a month to buy on a contract running twenty-five to thirty-five years.

KHRUSHCHEV: We have steel workers and we have peasants who also can afford to spend $14,000 for a house. Your American houses are built to last only 20 years so builders could sell new houses at the end. We build firmly. We build for our children and grandchildren.

NIXON: American houses last for more than 20 years, but even so, after twenty years, many Americans want a new house or a new kitchen. Their kitchen is obsolete by that time. . . . The American system is designed to take advantage of new inventions and new techniques.

KHRUSHCHEV: This theory does not hold water. Some things never get out of date—houses, for instance, and furniture, furnishings—perhaps—but not houses. I have read much about America and American houses, and I do not think that this exhibit and what you say is strictly accurate.

NIXON: Well, um . . .

KHRUSHCHEV: I hope I have not insulted you.

NIXON: I have been insulted by experts. Everything we say is in good humor. Always speak frankly.

KHRUSHCHEV: The Americans have created their own image of the Soviet man and think he is as you want him to be. But he is not as you think. You think the Russian people will be dumbfounded to see these things, but the fact is that newly built Russian houses have all this equipment right now.

NIXON: Yes, but . . .

KHRUSHCHEV: In Russia, all you have to do to get a house is to be born in the Soviet Union. You are entitled to housing. . . In America, if you don't have a dollar you have a right to choose between sleeping in a house or on the pavement. Yet you say we are the slave to Communism.

NIXON: I appreciate that you are very articulate and energetic.

KHRUSHCHEV: Energetic is not the same thing as wise.

NIXON: If you were in the Senate, we would call you a filibuster. You—[Khrushchev interrupts]—do all the talking and don't let anyone else talk. This exhibit was not designed to astound but to interest. Diversity, the right to choose, the fact that we have 1,000 builders building 1,000 different houses is the most important thing. We don't have one decision made at the top by one government official. This is the difference.

KHRUSHCHEV: On politics, we will never agree with you. For instance, Mikoyan likes very peppery soup. I do not. But this does not mean that we do not get along.

NIXON: You can learn from us, and we can learn from you. There must be a free exchange. Let the people choose the kind of house, the kind of soup, the kind of ideas that they want. . . .

KHRUSHCHEV: Don't you have a machine that puts food in the mouth and pushes it down? Many things you've shown us are interesting but they are not needed in life. They have no useful purpose. They are merely gadgets. We have a saying: if you have bedbugs you have to catch one and pour boiling water into the ear.

NIXON: We have another saying. This is that the way to kill a fly is to make it drink whiskey. But we have better use for whiskey. [aside] I like to have this battle of wits with the Chairman. He knows his business.

KHRUSHCHEV: [uninterested in data processing machine that answers questions about the United States] I have heard of your engineers. I am well aware of what they can do. You know for launching our missiles we need lots of calculating machines.

NIXON: [hearing jazz music] I don't like jazz music.

KHRUSHCHEV: I don't like it either.

NIXON: But my girls like it. . . .

KHRUSHCHEV: [He sees Nixon admiring the young models] You are for the girls, too.

NIXON: [changes the subject, indicating a vacuum cleaner] You don't need a wife.

We do not claim to astonish the Russian people. We hope to show our diversity and our right to choose. We do not wish to have decisions made at the top by government officials who say that all homes should be built in the same way. Would it not be better to compete in the relative merits of washing machines than in the strengths of rockets? Is this the kind of competition you want?

KHRUSHCHEV: Yes, that's the kind of competition we want. But your generals say: "Let's compete in rockets. We are strong and we can beat you." But in this respect we can also show you something.

NIXON: To me you are strong and we are strong. In some ways, you are stronger than we are. In others, we are stronger. We are both strong not only from the standpoint of weapons but from the standpoint of will and spirit. Neither should use the strength to put the other in a position where he in effect has an ultimatum. In this day and age that misses the point. With modern weapons it does not make a difference if war comes. We both have had it.

KHRUSHCHEV: For the fourth time I have to say I cannot recognize my friend Mr. Nixon. If all Americans agree with you, then who don't we agree [with]? This is what we want.

NIXON: Anyone who believes the American government does not reflect the people is not an accurate observer of the American scene. I hope the Prime Minster understands all the implications of what I have just said. Whenever you place either one of the powerful nations or any other in a position so that it has no choice but to accept dictation or fight, then you are playing with the most destructive force in the world. This is very important in the present world context. It's very dangerous. When we sit down at a conference table it cannot all be one way. One side cannot put an ultimatum to another. It is impossible. But I shall talk to you about this later.

10.

Opening Statement, The Great Debate: Kennedy v. Nixon (September 26, 1960)

Nixon did less well in his next debate, with his Democratic opponent for the presidency. Eager to establish a statesmanlike image, he hung back as his dashing former senate colleague sandbagged him. Kennedy twisted what was supposed to be the first debate's topic—domestic issues—into a stinging rebuke of America's international position. Plodding Nixon, having unilaterally disarmed himself of his usual slashing style—and exhausted from an unnecessarily punishing campaign schedule—defensively, almost pathetically, "subscribe[d] completely to the spirit that Senator Kennedy has expressed tonight," granting his arguments almost point by point or getting bogged down in a lumpy mass of technicalities.

There was, too, the single bead of sweat that broke out on Nixon's chin, and the infamous five o'clock shadow. It was JFK's show.

Mr. Smith, Senator Kennedy. The things that Senator Kennedy has said many of us can agree with. There is no question but that we cannot discuss our internal affairs in the United States without recognizing that they have a tremendous bearing on our international position. There is no question but that this nation cannot stand still; because we are in a deadly competition, a competition not only with the men in the Kremlin, but the men in Peking. We're ahead in this competition, as Senator Kennedy, I think, has implied. But when you're in a race, the only way to stay ahead is to move ahead. And I subscribe completely to the spirit that Senator Kennedy has expressed tonight, the spirit that the United States should move ahead.

Where, then, do we disagree?

I think we disagree on the implication of his remarks tonight and on the statements that he has made on many occasions during his campaign to the effect that the United States has been standing still.

We heard tonight, for example, the statement made that our growth in national product last year was the lowest of any industrial nation in the world.

Now last year, of course, was 1958. That happened to be a recession year. But when we look at the growth of G.N.P. this year, a year of recovery, we find that it's six and nine-tenths per cent and one of the highest in the world today. More about that later.

Looking then to this problem of how the United States should move ahead and where the United States is moving, I think it is well that we take the advice of a very famous campaigner: "Let's look at the record."

Is the United States standing still?

Is it true that this Administration, as Senator Kennedy has charged, has been an Administration of retreat, of defeat, of stagnation?

Is it true that, as far as this country is concerned, in the field of electric power, in all of the fields that he has mentioned, we have not been moving ahead?

Well, we have a comparison that we can make. We have the record of the Truman Administration of seven and a half years and the seven and a half years of the Eisenhower Administration.

When we compare these two records in the areas that Senator Kennedy has—has discussed tonight, I think we find that America has been moving ahead.

Let's take schools. We have built more schools in these last seven and a half years than we built in the previous seven and a half, for that matter in the previous twenty years.

Let's take hydroelectric power. We have developed more hydroelectric power in these seven and a half years than was developed in any previous administration in history.

Let us take hospitals. We find that more have been built in this Administration than in the previous Administration. The same is true of highways.

Let's put it in terms that all of us can understand.

We often hear gross national product discussed and in that respect may I say that when we compare the growth in this Administration with that of the previous Administration that then there was a total growth of eleven percent over seven years; in this Administration there has been a total growth of nineteen per cent over seven years.

That shows that there's been more growth in this Administration than in its predecessor. . . .

What kind of programs are we for?

We are for programs that will expand educational opportunities, that will give to all Americans their equal chance for education, for all of the things which are necessary and dear to the hearts of our people.

We are for programs, in addition, which will see that our medical care for the aged are—is—are much—is much better handled than it is at the present time. . . .

The final point that I would like to make is this: Senator Kennedy has suggested in his speeches that we lack compassion for the poor, for the old, and for others that are unfortunate.

Let us understand throughout this campaign that his motives and mine are sincere. I know what it means to be poor. I know what it means to see people who are unemployed.

I know Senator Kennedy feels as deeply about these problems as I do, but our disagreement is not about the goals for America but only about the means to reach those goals.

IV. Comeback

11.

“Gentlemen, this is my last press conference” (November 6, 1962)

Richard Nixon’s humiliation at the hands of John F. Kennedy would haunt him for the rest of his life. His attempt at a political comeback began with his memoir, Six Crises *(the crises were the Hiss Case, his Senate run against Helen Gahagan Douglas, the “secret fund” controversy, Eisenhower’s 1955 heart attack, the South America trip, the “Kitchen Debate,” and the campaign against Kennedy). The book was impressive, even-tempered, and introspective—but also veered off at points into an unhinged nursing of grievances real and imagined. “For the next twelve years of my public service in Washington, I was to be subjected to an utterly unprincipled and vicious smear campaign. Bigamy, forgery, drunkenness, thievery, anti-Semitism, perjury, the whole gamut of misconduct in public office,” went his conclusion to the Hiss chapter. The book was supposed to pave the way to his comeback in his run for California governor. But he lost that too—an extraordinary comedown for a man who had come within inches of the presidency. His concession speech to the press displayed Nixon at his most self-pitying worst. It was followed, not long after, by an ABC special entitled “The Political Obituary of Richard Nixon”—which featured as a commentator the suspected Communist and convicted perjurer Alger Hiss, doing better in polite society than the man who put him in jail.*

Good morning, gentlemen. Now that Mr. Klein has made his statement and now that all members of the press are so delighted that I have lost, I'd like to make a statement of my own.

. . . I appreciate the press coverage of this campaign. I think each of you covered it the way you saw it. You had to write it in the way according to your belief on how it would go. I don't believe publishers should tell reporters to write one way or another. I want them all to be free. I don't believe the FCC or anybody else should silence [word lost in transmission].

I have no complaints about the press coverage. I think each of you was writing it as you believed it. I congratulate Governor Brown, as Herb Klein has already indicated, for his victory. He has, I think the greatest honor and the greatest responsibility of any governor in the United States. And if he has this honor and this responsibility, I think that he will now have certainly a position of tremendous interest for America and as well as for the people of California.

I wish him well. I wish him well not only from my personal standpoint, because there were never on my part any personal considerations. I believe Governor Brown has a heart, even though he believes I do not. I believe he is a good American, even though he feels I am not. And therefore he is a good American, even though he feels I am not. And therefore I wish him well because he is the governor of the first state. He won, and I want this state to be led with courage. I want it to be led decisively and I want it to be led, certainly, with the assurance that the man who lost the campaign never during the course of the campaign raised a personal consideration against his opponent—never allowed any words indicating that his opponent was motivated by lack of heart or lack of patriotism to pass his lips.

I am proud of the fact that I defended my opponent's patriotism. You gentlemen didn't report it, but I am proud that I did it. I am proud also that I defended the fact that he was a man of good motives, a man that I disagreed with very strongly, but a man of good motives. I want that—for once, gentlemen—I would appreciate if you would write what I say, in that respect. I think it's very important that you write it. In the lead. In the lead.

Now, I don't mean by that, incidentally, all of you. There's one reporter here who has religiously, when he was covering me—and incidentally, this is no reflection on the others, because some of you, you know, weren't bothered. One reporter, Carl Greenberg—he's the only reporter on the [Los Angeles] *Times* that fits this thing, who wrote every word I said. He wrote it fairly. He wrote it objectively. I don't mean that others didn't have a right to do it differently. But Carl, despite whatever feeling he had, felt that he had an obligation to report the facts as he saw them.

I say these things about the press because I understand that was one of the things you were particularly interested in. There'll be no questions at this point on that score. I'll be glad to answer other questions. . . .

What will happen in Cuba? Can we allow this cancer of Communism to stay there? Is there a deal with regard to NATO? Is there going to be with regard to NATO and the Warsaw Pact? Are we going to continue any kind of an agreement in Cuba, which means that Khrushchev got what we said we would never agree to before he made his threat with regard to his missiles and that is, in effect, ringing down an Iron Curtain around Cuba? Those are the things that Mr. Kennedy, of course, will have to face up to, and I just hope—and I'm confident that if he has his own way he will face up to them, if he can only get those who opposed atomic tests, who want him to admit Red China to the UN, all of the woollyheads around him—if he can just keep them away from him and stand strong and firm with that good Irish fight of his, America will be in good shape in foreign policy. . . .

One last thing: What are my plans? Well, my plans are to go home. I'm going to get acquainted with my family again. And my plans, incidentally, are, from a political standpoint, of course, to take a holiday. It will be a long holiday. I don't say that with any sadness. I couldn't feel, frankly, more, well, frankly, proud of my staff for the campaign they helped me put on. We campaigned against great odds. We fought a good fight. We didn't win. And I take responsibility for any of my mistakes. As far as they're concerned, they're magnificent people, and I hope whoever next runs in California will look at my staff and take some of these people—use them—because they are—they're great political properties, shall we say, putting it in the—in a very materialistic way.

One last thing: People say, "What about the past? What about losing in '60 and losing in '64 [*sic*]? I remember somebody on my last television program said, 'Mr. Nixon, isn't it a comedown, having run for President, and almost made it, to run for governor?' The answer is I'm proud to have run for governor. Now, I would have liked to have won. But not having won, the main thing was that I battled—battled for the things I believed in. I did not win. I have no hard feelings against anybody, against my opponents and least of all the people of California. We got our message through as well as we could. The Cuban thing did not enable us to get it through in the two critical weeks that we wanted to, but nevertheless we got it through, and it is the people's choice.

They have chosen Mr. Brown. They have chosen his leadership, and I can only hope that that leadership will now become more decisive, that it will move California ahead and, so that America can move ahead—economically, morally, and spiritually—so that we can have character and self-reliance in this country. This is what we need to move forward.

One last thing. At the outset I said a couple of things with regard to the press that I noticed some of you looked a little irritated about. And my philosophy with regard to the press has never really gotten through. And I want it to get through. This cannot be said for any other American political figure today, I guess. Never in my sixteen years of campaigning have I complained to a publisher, to an editor, about the coverage of a reporter. I believe a reporter has got a right to write it as he feels it. I believe if a reporter believes that one man ought to win rather than the other, whether it's on television or radio or the like, he ought to say so. I will say to the reporter that I think, "Well, look, I wish you'd give my opponent the same going over that you give me."

And as I leave the press, all I can say is this: for sixteen years, ever since the Hiss case, you've had a lot of fun—a lot of fun—that you've had an opportunity to attack me and I think I've given as good as I've taken. I was carried right up to the last day. I made a talk on television, a talk in which

I made a flub—one of the few that I make, not because I'm so good on television but because I've been doing it a long time. I made a flub in which I said I was running for governor of the United States. The *Los Angeles Times* dutifully reported that. Mr. Brown the last day made a flub—a flub, incidentally, to the great credit of television, that was reported—I don't say this bitterly—in which he said, "I hope everybody wins. You vote the straight Democratic ticket, including Senator Kuchel." I was glad to hear him say it, because I was for Kuchel all the way. The *Los Angeles Times* did not report it. I think that it's time that our great newspapers have at least the same objectivity, the same fullness of coverage, that television has. And I can only say thank God for television and radio for keeping the newspapers a little honest.

Now some newspapers don't fall in the category to which I have spoken, but I can only say that the great metropolitan newspapers in this field, they have a right to take every position they want on the editorial page, but on the news page they also have a right to have reporters cover men who have strong feelings, whether they're for or against a candidate. But the responsibility also is to put a few Greenbergs on, on the candidate they happen to be against, whether they're against him on the editorial page or just philosophically deep down, a fellow who at least will report what the man says. That's all anybody can ask. . . .

The last play. I leave you gentlemen now, and you will write it. You will interpret. That's your right. But as I leave you I want you to know—just think how much you're going to be missing. You won't have Nixon to kick around anymore, because, gentlemen, this is my last press conference, and it will be the one in which I have welcomed the opportunity to test wits with you. I have always respected you. I have sometimes disagreed with you. But unlike some people, I've never cancelled a subscription to a paper, and also I never will.

I believe in reading what my opponents say, and I hope that what I have said today will at least make television, radio, and the press, first recognize the great responsibility they have to report all the news and, second, recognize that they have a right and a responsibility, if they're against a candidate, give him the shaft, but also recognize if they give him the shaft, put one lonely reporter on the campaign who will report what the candidate says now and then. Thank you, gentlemen, and good day.

12.

"The irresponsible tactics of some of the extreme civil rights leaders" (February 12, 1964)

On February 11, 1964, Alabama's segregationist governor George Wallace gave a barn-burning speech in Cincinnati excoriating civil rights leaders who had staged a one-day boycott of racially segregated schools in Northern cities. Richard Nixon, speaking in Cincinnati the very next day, detoured from his conventional dressing-down of Johnson administration foreign policy into a more polite recapitulation of Wallace's themes, calling the boycott "mob rule"—a bad-cop/good-cop continuity between Wallace's and Nixon's rhetoric on race and "law and order" that would persist for over eight more years. Nixon, who had always been a moderate supporter of civil rights, was shifting his ideological orientation rightward in preparation for a possible run against Barry Goldwater for the Republican presidential nomination, and foreshadowing a hot-button issue of the 1970s: "busing"—which Nixon says would "haul [children] from one school to another in order to force integration in an artificial and unworkable manner."

. . . A significant bi-partisan civil rights law will be enacted by the Congress next month, due in large part to the statesmanlike leadership of Congressman Bill McCulloch of Ohio.

If this law is effectively administered, it will be a great step forward in the struggle for equality of opportunity for all Americans.

But much of the good that the law will do will be destroyed if the irresponsible tactics of some of the extreme civil rights leaders continue.

A law is only as good as the will of the people to keep it. The hate engendered by demonstrators and boycotts has set Americans against Americans and has created an atmosphere of hate and distrust which, if it continues to grow, will make a new law a law in name only.

It is time for responsible civil rights leaders to take over from the extremists.

In this election year Republicans will be urged by some to outpromise the Johnson Administration on civil rights in the hope of political gain. I am completely opposed to this kind of political demagoguery. Making promises that can't be kept—raising hopes that can't be realized—are the cruelest hoaxes that can be perpetrated on a minority group that has suffered from such tactics for a hundred years.

I think that the Republican Party should stand forthrightly on these principles.

1. We are proud of our record from the time of Abraham Lincoln to the passage of the first civil

rights legislation in a hundred years under President Eisenhower.

2. We shall continue to lead the fight for equality under the law for all Americans, including not only our Negro citizens but other minorities who because their numbers are less are sometimes overlooked—the Puerto Ricans, the Eastern and Southern Europeans, the Central and South Americans, the Mexicans, and our American Indians.

3. But we are a Party that was founded on the principle of the rule of law. Abraham Lincoln led the nation to war to maintain the rule of law in our land.

4. The encouragement of disrespect for law through mass demonstrations, boycotts, and violation of property rights, in the long run, harms rather than helps the cause of civil rights. Some justify such tactics on the ground that they may hasten the passage of laws. But, at the same time, these tactics destroy the will of the people to obey those laws.

5. We disapprove of the spectacle of public officials lending the prestige of their office to extralegal pressures on the part of any minority or majority group. This encouragement of disregard for law and for the rights of other people and other minorities will plague the cause of better understanding among the American people for years to come. It negates or makes suspect the right of peti-

tion, the right of peaceful assembly, and the orderly process of law.

6. We stand for the rule of law and reject mob rule.

7. The only rights worth having are the rights created in the law, by lawful means, and which exist for all Americans equally and equitably.

8. We reject the idea that the way to reduce high Negro unemployment is to increase white unemployment. We stand for a program that will increase job opportunities for all Americans.

9. We oppose segregation in our schools either by law or in fact. But this problem must be dealt with in an orderly transition. We believe it is detrimental to both Negro and white children to uproot them from their communities and to haul them from one school to another in order to force integration in an artificial and unworkable manner.

10. Now that a new civil rights law will soon become a reality, we need a national program which will increase understanding among our people, the will to obey that law and other laws, and which will reduce the hate fomented by professional extremists and political demagogues.

13.

"Appraisal from Manila" (November 4, 1966)

Nixon spent the fall of 1966 baiting Lyndon Johnson over the president's frustrations in Vietnam. The coup de grace came when Johnson returned from a conference in Manila with South Vietnam's president Ngo Cao Ky. Nixon released a statement twisting a boilerplate diplomatic throwaway line in the Johnson-Ky communiqué about what would happen when the allies' war aim of a Communist-free South Vietnam was achieved—that American troops could withdraw after six months—into a design for "mutual withdrawal," a dastardly offer of surrender. Johnson, outraged, attacked Nixon viciously at a White House press conference. Out of the confrontation, Nixon succeeded in getting some in the media to frame the 1966 congressional elections as a referendum over Nixon's position on Vietnam versus President Johnson's, and the spectacular success of Republicans as a Nixon accomplishment—even though the Republicans' success had much more to do with backlash over race riots.

In one significant respect the President's visit to Manila has served a useful purpose. It has helped to unite our Asian allies and to give Asians a visible demonstration that America remains behind her commitment to a free Pacific.

Every American can take pride as well in the warm reception accorded their President in the many foreign capitals he visited.

It is time now, however, to take stock of what Manila accomplished. It is time to renew the debate on the Johnson Administration's policy in Vietnam, for this war is not only the global issue in this election, it is one of the central issues of our time.

On his return, the President said that he did not seek nor did he receive any new commitments. A number of foreign policy observers have pointed out that the trip has brought us no closer to peace.

In fact, the wording of the communiqué itself has raised some grave policy questions which should be answered by President Johnson before the American people go to the polls on November 8.

1. The Peace Proposal—Mutual Withdrawal

The Manila communiqué states: "The people of South Vietnam will ask their allies to remove their forces and evacuate their installations as the military and subversive forces of North Vietnam are withdrawn, infiltration ceases, and the level of violence thus subsides."

This states clearly that if North Vietnam withdraws its forces back across its border, and the violence thus subsides, we shall withdraw all American forces out of Vietnam, most of them 10,000 miles back to the United States. The effect of this mutual withdrawal would be to leave the fate of South Vietnam to the Vietcong and the South Vietnamese Army.

On the surface, a commitment to mutual withdrawal appears to be a reasonable approach toward de-escalation. But, on reflection, mutual withdrawal of North Vietnam and United States troops simply turns back the clock two years and says "let the South Vietnamese fight it out with the Vietcong."

The South Vietnamese Army could not prevail for any length of time over the Communist guerrillas without American advisers, air support and logistical backing. Communist victory would most certainly be the result of "mutual withdrawal" if the North Vietnamese continued their own logistical support of the Communist guerillas.

At the moment, the major area where Vietcong terrorists face South Vietnamese troops without large commitments of either U.S. or North Vietnamese troops is in the Mekong Delta; there the Vietcong hold the upper hand. Thus, the first question which should be answered by the President is:

Does this new Manila proposal for mutual withdrawal by the U.S. and North Vietnam mean that we are now willing to stand aloof and let the future of the South Vietnamese be determined by the victor of a military contest between the Vietcong and the Government of South Vietnam?

If this is the proper interpretation of the Manila communiqué, our endorsement jeopardizes every strategic American objective in Vietnam. . . .

In my travels across the country in recent months, we have encountered an odd sense of helplessness on the part of many thoughtful Americans in the field of foreign policy.

Their frustration is caused by a combination of lack of information, a cacophony of voices that purport to speak for United States policy, a confusion of goals and a lack of answers to legitimate questions such as those posed in this appraisal.

Informed debate on the conduct of the war is well within the tradition of the bipartisan foreign policy, so carefully built over the past three decades.

After the orderly tumult over an American election is over, and the people have determined the nature of the Congress, it would be constructive for the President to call together leaders of both parties to pursue together the development of a clear, practical, bipartisan foreign policy that will end the war and provide the basis for a lasting peace.

14.

"What Has Happened to America?" (*Reader's Digest*, October 1967)

Beginning in the mid-1960s, after a long period of liberal and Democratic control of all three branches of government, signs of disorder saturated American society. Crime rates were skyrocketing; young people were turning their back on traditional norms, protesting the Vietnam War, and contesting the moral legitimacy of their elders; and, most dramatically, each new summer seemed to augur yet more dramatic riots in the nation's black ghettos. In the summer of 1967, twenty-six died in riots in Newark, New Jersey, and forty-two in Detroit. Richard Nixon, always a stickler for order, made a bid for the support of Americans who feared society was coming apart at the seams a key part of his political appeal going into the 1968 presidential election. This article in the nation's most widely read monthly, Reader's Digest*—whose publisher was a strong Nixon backer and friend—added a characteristically Nixonian touch: he seemed to put more of the blame on the indulgence of know-it-all sophisticates than on the people actually committing the crimes.*

Just three years ago this nation seemed to be completing its greatest decade of racial progress and entering one of the most hopeful periods in American history. Twenty million Negroes were at last being admitted to full membership in the society, and this social miracle was being performed with a minimum of friction and without loss of our freedom or tranquility.

With this star of racial peace and progress before us, how did it happen that last summer saw the United States blazing in an inferno of urban anarchy?

In more than 20 cities police and mayors were unable to cope with armed insurrection. Central cities were abandoned to snipers, looters and arsonists. Only the state militia or federal soldiers could regain the city and restore peace. . . .

Why is it that in a few short years a nation which enjoys the freedom and material abundance of America has become among the most lawless and violent in the history of free peoples?

There has been a tendency in this country to charge off the violence and the rioting of the past summer solely to the deep racial division between Negro and white. Certainly racial animosities—and agonies—were the most visible causes. But riots were also the most virulent symptoms to date of another, and in some ways graver, national disorder—the decline in respect for public authority and the rule of law in America. Far from being a great society, ours is becoming a lawless society.

Slipping Standards

The symptoms are everywhere manifest: in the public attitude toward police, in the mounting traffic in illicit drugs, in the volume of teen-age arrests, in campus disorders and the growth of white-collar crime. The fact that whites looted happily along with Negroes in Detroit is ample proof that the affliction is not confined to one race.

The shocking crime and disorder in American life today flow in large measure from two fundamental changes that have occurred in the attitudes of many Americans.

First, there is the permissiveness toward violation of the law and public order by those who agree with the cause in question. Second, there is the indulgence of crime because of sympathy for the past grievances of those who have become criminals.

Our judges have gone too far in weakening the peace forces as against the criminal forces.

Our opinion-makers have gone too far in promoting the doctrine that when a law is broken, society, not the criminal, is to blame.

Our teachers, preachers, and politicians have gone too far in advocating the idea that each individual should determine what laws are good and what laws are bad, and that he then should obey the law he likes and disobey the law he dislikes.

Thus we find that many who oppose the war in Vietnam excuse or ignore or even applaud those who protest that war by disrupting parades, invading government offices, burning draft cards, blocking troop trains or desecrating the American flag.

The same permissiveness is applied to those who defy the law in pursuit of civil rights. This trend has gone so far in America that there is not only a growing tolerance of lawlessness but an increasing public acceptance of civil disobedience. Men of intellectual and moral eminence who encourage public disobedience of the law are responsible for the acts of those who inevitably follow their counsel: the poor, the ignorant and the impressionable. For example, to the professor objecting to de facto segregation, it may be crystal clear where civil disobedience may begin and where it must end. But the boundaries have become fluid to his students and other listeners. Today in the urban slums, the limits of responsible action are all but invisible. . . .

There is little question that our judicial and legal system provides more safeguards against the conviction of an innocent man than any other legal system on earth. We should view this accomplishment with pride, and we must preserve it. But the first responsibility of government and a primary responsibility of the judicial system is to guarantee to each citizen his primary civil right—the right to be protected from domestic violence. In recent years our system has failed dismally in this responsibility—and it cannot redeem itself by pointing to the conscientious manner in which it treats suspected criminals. . . .

Any system that fashions its safe-guards for the innocent so broadly and haphazardly that they also provide haven from punishment for uncounted thousands of the guilty is a failure—an indictment, not an adornment, of a free society. No need is more urgent today than the need to strengthen the peace forces as against the criminal forces that are at large in America.

Midsummer Madness

The nationwide deterioration of respect for authority, the law and civil order reached its peak this past summer when mobs in 100 cities burned and looted and killed in a senseless attack upon their society, its agents and its law.

We should make no mistake. This country cannot temporize or equivocate in this showdown with anarchy; to do so is to risk our freedoms first and then our society and nation as we know it. . . .

The problems of our great cities were decades in building; they will be decades in their solution.

While attacking the problems with urgency we must await the results with patience. But we cannot have patience with urban violence. Immediate and decisive force must be the first response. For there can be no progress unless there is an end to violence and unless there is respect for the rule of law. To ensure the success of long-range programs, we must first deal with the immediate crisis—the riots.

An End to Violence

How are riots to be prevented?

The first step is better pay and better training and higher standards for police; we must attract the highest caliber of individual to the force. . . .

Second, there must be a substantial upgrading in the number of police. The first purpose of the added manpower is to bring the physical presence of the law into those communities where the writ of authority has ceased to run.

The responsibility of the police in these areas is not only to maintain the peace but to protect life and property. It is the Negro citizens who suffer most from radical violence. When police and firemen retreat under sniper fire from riot-torn districts to let them "burn out," it is the Negro's district that is burned out. . . .

There can be no right to revolt in this society; no right to demonstrate outside the law, and, in

Lincoln's words, "no grievance that is a fit object of redress by mob law." In a civilized nation no man can excuse his crime against the person or property of another by claiming that he, too, has been a victim of injustice. To tolerate that is to invite anarchy. . . .

To heal the wounds that have torn the nation asunder, to re-establish respect for law and the principles that have been the source of America's growth and greatness will require the example of leaders in every walk of American life. More important than that, it will require the wisdom, the patience and the personal commitment of every American.

15.

"Asia after Viet Nam" (*Foreign Affairs*, October 1967)

This article foreshadowed President Nixon's foreign policy innovations in two important respects. First was his recognition of the American public's likely unwillingness to support another war against "externally supported communist insurrection." He thus advises: "other nations must recognize that the role of the United States as world policeman is likely to be limited in the future." He said much the same thing two years later, in enunciating the "Nixon Doctrine" on July 25, 1969: that "except for the threat of a major power involving nuclear weapons," future defenses will need to be undertaken by "the Asian nations themselves." The second foreshadowing involved China, which American policy-makers had sought to isolate as an international pariah for almost two decades. "Taking the long view," Nixon argued, "we simply cannot afford to leave China forever outside the family of nations, there to nurture its fantasies, cherish its hates and threaten its neighbors."

I

The war in Viet Nam has for so long dominated our field of vision that it has distorted our picture of Asia. A small country on the rim of the continent has filled the screen of our minds; but it does not fill the map. Sometimes dramatically, but more often quietly, the rest of Asia has been undergoing a profound, an exciting and on balance an extraordinarily promising transformation. One key to this transformation is the development of a number of the Asian economies; another is gathering disaffection with all the old isms that have so long imprisoned so many minds and so many governments. By and large the non-communist Asian governments are looking for solutions that work, rather than the solutions that fit a preconceived set of doctrines and dogmas.

Most them also recognize a common danger, and see its source as Peking. Taken together, these developments present an extraordinary set of opportunities for a U.S. policy which must begin to look beyond Viet Nam. In looking forward to the future, however, we should not ignore the vital role Viet Nam has played in making these developments possible. Whatever one may think of the "domino" theory, it is beyond question that without the American commitment in Viet Nam Asia would be a far different place today.

The U.S. presence has provided tangible and highly visible proof that communism is not necessarily the wave of Asia's future. This was a vital factor in the turnaround in Indonesia, where a tendency toward fatalism is a national characteristic. It provided a shield behind which the anti-communist forces found the courage and the capacity to stage their counter-coup and, at the final moment, to rescue their country from the Chinese orbit. And, with its 100 million people, and its 3,000-mile arc of islands containing the region's richest hoard of natural resources, Indonesia constitutes by far the greatest prize in the Southeast Asian area.

Beyond this, Viet Nam has diverted Peking from such other potential targets as India, Thailand and Malaysia. It has bought vitally needed time for governments that were weak or unstable or leaning toward Peking as a hedge against the future—time which has allowed them to attempt to cope with their own insurrections while pressing ahead with their political, economic, and military development. From Japan to India, Asian leaders know why we are in Viet Nam and, privately if not publicly, they urge us to see it through to a satisfactory conclusion.

II

Many argue that an Atlantic axis is natural and necessary, but maintain, in effect, that Kipling was right, and that the Asian peoples are so "different" that Asia itself is only peripherally an American concern. This represents a racial and cultural chauvinism that does little credit to American ideals, and it shows little appreciation either of the westward thrust of American interests or of the dynamics of world development.

During the final third of the twentieth century, Asia, not Europe or Latin America, will pose the greatest danger of a confrontation which could escalate into World War III. At the same time, the fact that the United States has now fought three Asian wars in the space of a generation is grimly but truly symbolic of the deepening involvement of the United States in what happens on the other side of the Pacific—which modern transportation and communication have brought closer to us today than Europe was in the years immediately preceding World War II.

The United States is a Pacific power. Europe has been withdrawing the remnants of empire, but the United States, with its coast reaching in an arc from Mexico to the Bering Straits, is one anchor of a vast Pacific community. Both our interests and our ideals propel us westward across the Pacific, not as conquerors but as partners, linked by the sea not only with those oriental nations on Asia's Pacific littoral but at the same time with occidental Australia and New Zealand, and the island nations in between.

Since World War II, a new Asia has been emerging with startling rapidity; indeed, Asia is changing more swiftly than any other part of the world. All around the rim of China nations are becoming Western without ceasing to be Asian.

The dominant development in Asia immediately after World War II was decolonization, with its admixture of intense nationalism. But the old nationalist slogans have less meaning for today's young than they had for their fathers. Having never known a "colonialist," they find colonialists unconvincing as scapegoats for the present ills of their societies. If dissatisfied with conditions as they see them, the young tend to blame those now in power.

As the sharp anticolonial focus blurs, the old nationalism is evolving into a more complex, multi-layered set of concepts and attitudes. On the one hand are a multitude of local and tribal identifications—the Montagnards in Viet Nam, the Han tribes in Burma, the provincial and linguistic separatisms that currently claw at the fabric of Indian unity. On the other hand, there is a reaching-out by the governing élites, and particularly the young, for something larger, more like an Asian regionalism.

The developing coherence of Asian regional thinking is a disposition to consider problems and loyalties in regional terms, and to evolve regional approaches to development needs and to the evolution of a new world order. This is not excessively chauvinistic, but rather in the nature of a coalescing confidence, a recognition that Asia can become a counterbalance to the West, and an increasing disposition to seek Asian solutions to Asian problems through cooperative action.

Along with the rising complex of national, subregional and regional identification and pride, there is also an acute sense of common danger—a factor which serves as a catalyst to the others. The common danger from Communist China is now in the process of shifting the Asian governments' center of concern. During the colonial and immediately post-colonial eras, Asians stood opposed primarily to the West, which represented the intruding alien power. But now the West has abandoned its colonial role, and it no longer threatens the independence of the Asian nations. Red China, however, does, and its threat is clear, present and repeatedly and insistently expressed. The message has not been lost on Asia's leaders. They recognize that the West, and particularly the United States, now represents not an oppressor but a protector. And they recognize their need for protection.

This does not mean that the old resentments and distrusts have vanished, or that new ones will not arise. It does, however, mean that there has been an important shift in the balance of their perceptions about the balance of danger, and this shift has important implications for the future.

One of the legacies of Viet Nam almost certainly will be a deep reluctance on the part of the United States to become involved once again in a similar intervention on a similar basis. The war has imposed severe strains on the United States, not only militarily and economically but socially and politically as well. Bitter dissension has torn the fabric of American intellectual life, and whatever the outcome of the war the tear may be a long time mending. If another friendly country should be faced with an externally supported communist insurrection—whether in Asia, or in Africa or even Latin America—there is serious question whether the American public or the American Congress would now support a unilateral American intervention, even at the request of the host government. This makes it vitally in their own interest that the nations in the path of China's ambitions move quickly to establish an indigenous Asian framework for their own future security.

In doing so, they need to fashion arrangements able to deal both with old-style wars and with new—with traditional wars, in which armies cross over national boundaries, and with the so-called "wars of national liberation," in which they burrow under national boundaries.

I am not arguing that the day is past when the United States would respond militarily to communist threats in the less stable parts of the world, or that a unilateral response to a unilateral request for help is out of the question. But other nations must recognize that the role of the United States as world policeman is likely to be limited in the future. To ensure that a U.S. response will be forthcoming if needed, machinery must be created that is capable of meeting two conditions: (a) a collective effort by the nations of the region to contain the threat by themselves; and, if that effort fails, (b) a collective request to the United States for assistance. This is important not only from the respective national standpoints, but also from the standpoint of avoiding nuclear collision.

Nations not possessing great power can indulge in the luxury of criticism of others; those possessing it have the responsibility of decision. Faced with a clear challenge, the decision not to use one's power must be as deliberate as the decision to use it. The consequences can be fully as far-reaching and fully as irrevocable.

If another world war is to be prevented, every step possible must be taken to avert direct confrontations between the nuclear powers. To achieve this, it is essential to minimize the number of occasions on which the great powers have to decide whether or not to commit their forces. These choices cannot be eliminated, but they can be reduced by the development of regional defense pacts, in which nations undertake, among themselves, to attempt to contain aggression in their own areas.

If the initial response to a threatened aggression, of whichever type—whether across the border or under it—can be made by lesser powers in the immediate area and thus within the path of aggression, one of two things can be achieved: either they can in fact contain it by themselves, in which case the United States is spared involvement and thus the world is spared the consequences of great-power action; or, if they cannot, the ultimate choice can be presented to the United States in clear-cut terms, by nations which would automatically become allies in whatever response might prove necessary. To put it another way, the regional pact becomes a buffer separating the distant great power from the immediate threat. Only if the buffer proves insufficient does the great power become involved, and then in terms that make victory more attainable and the enterprise more palatable. . . .

III

Military security has to rest, ultimately, on economic and political stability. One of the effects of the rapidity of change in the world today is that there can no longer be static stability; there can only be dynamic stability. A nation or society that fails to keep pace with change is in danger of flying apart. It is important that we recognize this, but equally important that in trying to maintain a dynamic stability we remember that the stability is as important as the dynamism.

If a given set of ends is deemed desirable, then from the standpoint of those dedicated to peace and an essential stability in world order the desideratum is to reach those ends by evolutionary rather than revolutionary means. Looking at the pattern of change in non-communist Asia, we find that the professed aims of the revolutionaries are in fact being achieved by an evolutionary process. This offers a dramatic opportunity to draw the distinction between the fact of a revolutionary result and the process of revolutionary change. The Asian nations are showing that evolutionary change can be as exciting as revolutionary change. Having revolutionized the aims of their societies, they are showing what can be achieved within a framework of dynamic stability.

The "people," in the broadest sense, have become an entity to be served rather than used. In much of Asia, this change represents a revolution of no less magnitude than the revolution that created the industrial West, or that in the years following World War II transformed empires into new and struggling nations. It is precisely the promise of this reversal that has been at the heart of communist rhetoric, and at the heart of the popular and intellectual appeal which that rhetoric achieved.

Not all governments of non-communist Asia fit the Western ideal of parliamentary democracy—far from it. But Americans must recognize that a highly sophisticated, highly advanced political system, which required many centuries to develop in the West, may not be best for other nations which have far different traditions and still are in an earlier stage of development. What matters is that these governments are consciously, deliberately and programmatically developing in the direction of greater liberty, greater abundance, broader choice and increased popular involvement in the processes of government.

Poverty that was accepted for centuries as the norm is accepted no longer. In a sense it could be said that a new chapter is being written in the winning of the West: in this case, a winning of the promise of Western technology and Western organization by the nations of the East. The cultural clash has had its costs and produced its strains, but out of it is coming a modernization of ancient civilizations that promises to leap the centuries.

The process produces transitional anomalies—such as the Indian woman squatting in the mud, forming cow-dung patties with her hands and laying them out to dry, while a transistor radio in her lap plays music from a Delhi station. It takes a long time to bring visions of the future to the far villages—but time is needed to make those visions credible, and make them achievable. Too wide a gap between reality and expectation always produces an explosive situation, and the fact that what the leaders know is possible is unknown to the great mass of the peasantry helps buy time to make the possible achievable. But the important thing is that the leaders do know what is possible, and by and large they are determined to make it happen.

Whether that process is going to proceed at a pace fast enough to keep one step ahead of the pressure of rising expectations is one of the great questions and challenges of the years ahead. But there is solid ground for hope. The successful Asian nations have been writing extraordinary records. To call their performance an economic miracle would be something of a semantic imprecision; it would also be a disservice. Precisely because the origins and ingredients of that success are not miraculous, it offers hope to those which have not yet turned the corner.

India is still a staggering giant, Burma flirts with economic chaos, and the Philippines, caught in a conflict of cultures and in search of an identity, lives in a precarious economic and social balance. But the most exciting trends in economic development today are being recorded by those Asian nations that have accepted the keys of progress and used them. Japan, Hong Kong, Taiwan, Thailand,

Korea, Singapore and Malaysia all have been recording sustained economic growth rates of 7 percent a year or more; Japan has sustained a remarkable average of 9 percent a year since 1950, and an average 16.7 per year increase in exports over the same period. Thailand shifted into a period of rapid growth in 1958 and has averaged 7 percent a year since. South Korea, despite the unflattering estimates of its people's abilities by the average G.I. during the Korean War, is shooting ahead at a growth rate that has averaged 8 percent a year since 1963, with an average 42 percent a year increase in its exports.

These rapidly advancing countries vary widely in their social traditions and political systems, but their methods of economic management have certain traits in common: a prime reliance on private enterprise and on the pricing mechanisms of the market as the chief determinant of business decisions; a pacing of monetary expansion to match growth in output; receptivity to private capital investment, both domestic and foreign, including such incentives as tax advantages and quick government clearance of proposed projects; imaginative national programs for dealing with social problems; and, not least, a generally restrained posture in government planning, with the government's role suggestive rather than coercive. These nations have, in short, discovered and applied the lessons of America's own economic woes.

IV

. . . Any American policy toward Asia must come urgently to grips with the reality of China. This does not mean, as many would simplistically have it, rushing to grant recognition to Peking, to admit it to the United Nations and to ply it with offers of trade—all of which would serve to confirm its rulers in their present course. It does mean recognizing the present and potential danger from Communist China, and taking measures designed to meet that danger. It also means distinguishing carefully between long-range and short-range policies, and fashioning short-range programs so as to advance our long-range goals.

Taking the long view, we simply cannot afford to leave China forever outside the family of nations, there to nurture its fantasies, cherish its hates and threaten its neighbors. There is no place on this small planet for a billion of its potentially most able people to live in angry isolation. But we could go disastrously wrong if, in pursuing this long-range goal, we failed in the short range to read the lessons of history.

The world cannot be safe until China changes. Thus our aim, to the extent that we can influence events, should be to induce change. The way to do this is to persuade China that it must change: that it cannot satisfy its imperial ambitions, and that its own national interest requires a turning away from foreign adventuring and a turning inward toward the solution of its own domestic problems.

If the challenge posed by the Soviet Union after World War II was not precisely similar, it was sufficiently so to offer a valid precedent and a valuable lesson. Moscow finally changed when it, too, found that change was necessary. This was essentially a change of the head, not of the heart. Internal evolution played a role, to be sure, but the key factor was that the West was able to create conditions—notably in the shoring up of European defenses, the rapid restoration of European economies and the cementing of the Atlantic Alliance—that forced Moscow to look to the wisdom of reaching some measure of accommodation with the West. We are still far from reaching a full détente, but at least substantial progress has been made. . . .

Some counsel conceding to China a "sphere of influence" embracing much of the Asian mainland and extending even to the island nations beyond; others urge that we eliminate the threat of preemptive war. Clearly, neither of these courses would be acceptable to the United States or to its Asian allies. Others argue that we should seek an anti-Chinese alliance with European powers, even including the Soviet Union. Quite apart from the obvious problems involved in Soviet participation, such a course would inevitably carry connotations of Europe vs. Asia, white vs. non-white, which could have catastrophic repercussions throughout the rest of the non-white world in general and Asia in particular. If our long-range aim is to pull China back into the family of nations, we must avoid the impression that the great powers or the European powers are "ganging up"; the response should clearly be one of active defense rather than potential offense, and must be untainted with any suspicion of racism.

For the United States to go it alone in containing China would not only place an unconscionable burden on our own country, but also would heighten the chances of nuclear war while undercutting the independent development of the nations of Asia. The primary restraint on China's Asian ambitions should be exercised by the Asian nations in the path of those ambitions, backed by the ultimate power of the United States. This is sound strategically, sound psychologically and sound in terms of the dynamics of Asian development. Only as the nations of non-communist Asia become so strong—economically, politically, and militarily—that they no longer furnish tempting targets for Chinese aggression, will the leaders in Peking be persuaded to turn their energies inward rather than outward. And that will be the time when the dialogue with mainland China can begin.

For the short run, then, this means a policy of firm restraint, of no reward, of a creative counterpressure designed to persuade Peking that its interests can be served only by accepting the basic rules of international civility. For the long run, it means pulling China back into the world community—but as a great and progressing nation, not as the epicenter of world revolution.

"Containment without isolation" is a good phrase and a sound concept, as far as it goes. But it covers only half the problem. Along with it, we need a positive policy of pressure and persuading, of dynamic detoxification, a marshaling of Asian forces both to keep the peace and to help draw off the poison from the Thoughts of Mao.

Dealing with Red China is something like trying to cope with the more explosive ghetto elements of our own country. In each case a potentially destructive force has to be curbed; in each case, an outlaw element has to be brought within the law; in each case dialogues have to be opened; in each case aggression has to be restrained while education proceeds; and, not least, in neither case can we afford to let those now self-exiled from society stay exiled forever. We have to proceed with both an urgency born of necessity and a patience born of realism, moving by calculated steps toward the final goal. . . .

16.

"The first civil right of every American is to be free from domestic violence" (August 8, 1968)

Rhetorically, Nixon's speech accepting the Republican presidential nomination neatly cleaved the nation in two. On the one hand were the "shouters." They were responsible for "cities enveloped in smoke and flame," "sirens in the night," "Americans hating each other; fighting each other; killing each other at home." The other half were the victims of the first: "forgotten Americans," who "give steel to the backbone of America," who "work," "save," "pay their taxes," and "care." They were "the real voice of America"—a suggestion that America's growing population of protesters weren't real Americans at all.

For a few moments, let us look at America, let us listen to America. . . .

As we look at America, we see cities enveloped in smoke and flame.

We hear sirens in the night.

We see Americans dying on distant battlefields abroad.

We see Americans hating each other; fighting each other; killing each other at home.

And as we see and hear these things, millions of Americans cry out in anguish.

Did we come all this way for this?

Did American boys die in Normandy, and Korea, and in Valley Forge for this?

Listen to the answer to those questions.

It is another voice. It is the quiet voice in the tumult and the shouting.

It is the voice of the great majority of Americans, the forgotten Americans—the non-shouters; the non-demonstrators.

They are not racists or sick; they are not guilty of the crime that plagues the land.

They are black and they are white—they're native born and foreign born—they're young and they're old.

They work in America's factories.

They run America's businesses.

They serve in government.

They provide most of the soldiers who died to keep us free.

They give drive to the spirit of America.

They give lift to the American Dream.

They give steel to the backbone of America. They are good people, they are decent people; they work, and they save, and they pay their taxes, and they care.

Like Theodore Roosevelt, they know that this country will not be a good place for any of us to live in unless it is a good place for all of us to live in.

This I say to you tonight is the real voice of America. . . .

Now, there is no quarrel between progress and order—because neither can exist without the other.

So let us have order in America—not the order that suppresses dissent and discourages change but the order which guarantees the right to dissent and provides the basis for peaceful change.

And tonight, it is time for some honest talk about the problem of order in the United States.

Let us always respect, as I do, our courts and those who serve on them. But let us also recognize that some of our courts in their decisions have gone too far in weakening the peace forces as against the criminal forces in this country and we must act to restore that balance.

Let those who have the responsibility to enforce our laws and our judges who have the responsibility to interpret them be dedicated to the great principles of civil rights.

But let them also recognize that the first civil right of every American is to be free from domestic violence, and that right must be guaranteed in this country. . . .

Tonight, I see the face of a child.

He lives in a great city. He is black. Or he is white. He is Mexican, Italian, Polish. None of that matters. What matters, he's an American child.

That child in that great city is more important than any politician's promise. He is America. He is a poet. He is a scientist, he is a great teacher, he is a proud craftsman. He is everything we ever hoped to be and everything we dare to dream to be.

He sleeps the sleep of childhood and he dreams the dreams of a child.

And yet when he awakens, he awakens to a living nightmare of poverty, neglect and despair.

He fails in school.

He ends up on welfare.

For him the American system is one that feeds his stomach and starves his soul. It breaks his heart. And in the end it may take his life on some distant battlefield.

To millions of children in this rich land, this is their prospect of the future.

But this is only part of what I see in America.

I see another child tonight.

He hears the train go by at night and he dreams of faraway places where he'd like to go.

It seems like an impossible dream.

But he is helped on his journey through life.

A father who had to go to work before he finished the sixth grade, sacrificed everything he had so that his sons could go to college.

A gentle, Quaker mother, with a passionate concern for peace, quietly wept when he went to war but she understood why he had to go.

A great teacher, a remarkable football coach, an inspirational minister encouraged him on his way.

A courageous wife and loyal children stood by him in victory and also defeat.

And in his chosen profession of politics, first there were scores, then hundreds, then thousands, and finally millions worked for his success.

And tonight he stands before you—nominated for President of the United States of America.

You can see why I believe so deeply in the American Dream.

For most of us the American Revolution has been won; the American Dream has come true.

And what I ask you to do tonight is to help me make that dream come true for millions to whom it's an impossible dream today. . . .

My fellow Americans, the long dark night for America is about to end.

The time has come for us to leave the valley of despair and climb the mountain so that we may see the glory of the dawn—a new day for America, and a new dawn for peace and freedom in the world.

V. President

17.

"To lower our voices would be a simple thing" (inaugural address, January 20, 1969)

Nixon's first speech as president was hailed as a masterpiece of conciliation in dark times by the press, who took his pledge of open, honest government, "helping, caring, doing," at face value—once more declaring the dawn of a "new Nixon." The speech also folded in the cadences of the politician he resented most in the world: the late John F. Kennedy ("I do not offer a life of uninspiring ease . . . I ask you to join in a high adventure—one as rich as humanity itself, and exciting as the times we live in"). The media marked the return of the "old Nixon" with his June commencement speech at the Air Force Academy, an angry, resentful address in which he imputed cowardice to critics of the Vietnam War in "the so-called 'best circles,'" and deflected concerns about wasteful Pentagon spending with the imprecation, "It is open season on the Armed Forces."

. . . Each moment in history is a fleeting time, precious and unique. But some stand out as moments of beginning, in which courses are set that shape decades or centuries. This can be such a moment.

Forces now are converging that make possible, for the first time, the hope that many of man's deepest aspirations can at last be realized. The spiraling pace of change allows us to contemplate, within our own lifetime, advances that once would have taken centuries.

In throwing wide the horizons of space, we have discovered new horizons on earth.

For the first time, because the people of the world want peace, and the leaders of the world are afraid of war, the times are on the side of peace.

Eight years from now America will celebrate its 200th anniversary as a nation. Within the lifetime of most people now living, mankind will celebrate that great new year which comes only once in a thousand years—the beginning of the third millennium.

What kind of a nation we will be, what kind of a world we will live in, whether we shape the future in the image of our hopes, is ours to determine by our actions and our choices.

The greatest honor history can bestow is the title of peacemaker. This honor now beckons America—the chance to help lead the world at last out of the valley of turmoil and onto that high ground of peace that man has dreamed of since the dawn of civilization.

If we succeed, generations to come will say of us now living that we mastered our moment, that we helped make the world safe for mankind.

This is our summons to greatness.

I believe the American people are ready to answer this call.

The second third of this century has been a time of proud achievement. We have made enormous strides in science and industry and agriculture. We have shared our wealth more broadly than ever. We have learned at last to manage a modern economy to assure its continued growth.

We have given freedom new reach. We have begun to make its promise real for black as well as for white.

We see the hope of tomorrow in the youth of today. I know America's youth. I believe in them. We can be proud that they are better educated, more committed, more passionately driven by conscience than any generation in our history.

No people has ever been so close to the achievement of a just and abundant society, or so possessed of the will to achieve it. And because our strengths are so great, we can afford to appraise our weaknesses with candor and to approach them with hope.

Standing in this same place a third of a century ago, Franklin Delano Roosevelt addressed a nation ravaged by depression and gripped in fear. He could say in surveying the Nation's troubles: "They concern, thank God, only material things." Our crisis today is in reverse.

We find ourselves rich in goods, but ragged in spirit; reaching with magnificent precision for the moon, but failing into raucous discord on earth.

We are caught in war, wanting peace. We are torn by division, wanting unity. We see around us empty lives, wanting fulfillment. We see tasks that need doing, waiting for hands to do them.

To a crisis of the spirit, we need an answer of the spirit.

And to find that answer, we need only look within ourselves.

When we listen to "the better angels of our nature," we find that they celebrate the simple things, the basic things—such as goodness, decency, love, kindness.

Greatness comes in simple trappings. The simple things are the ones most needed today if we are to surmount what divides us, and cement what unites us.

To lower our voices would be a simple thing.

In these difficult years, America has suffered from a fever of words; from inflated rhetoric that promises more than it can deliver; from angry rhetoric that fans discontents into hatreds; from bombastic rhetoric that postures instead of persuading.

We cannot learn from one another until we stop shouting at one another—until we speak quietly enough so that our words can be heard as well as our voices.

For its part, government will listen. We will strive to listen in new ways—to the voices of quiet anguish, the voices that speak without words, the voices of the heart—to the injured voices, the anxious voices, the voices that have despaired of being heard.

Those who have been left out, we will try to bring in.

Those left behind, we will help to catch up.

For all of our people, we will set as our goal the decent order that makes progress possible and our lives secure.

As we reach toward our hopes, our task is to build on what has gone before—not turning away from the old, but turning toward the new.

In this past third of a century, government has passed more laws, spent more money, initiated more programs than in all our previous history.

In pursuing our goals of full employment, better housing, excellence in education; in rebuilding our cities and improving our rural areas; in protecting our environment and enhancing the quality of life—in all these and more, we will and must press urgently forward.

We shall plan now for the day when our wealth can be transferred from the destruction of war abroad to the urgent needs of our people at home.

The American dream does not come to those who fall asleep.

But we are approaching the limits of what government alone can do.

Our greatest need now is to reach beyond government, to enlist the legions of the concerned and the committed.

What has to be done, has to be done by government and people together or it will not be done at all. The lesson of past agony is that without the people we can do nothing—with the people we can do everything.

To match the magnitude of our tasks, we need the energies of our people—enlisted not only in grand enterprises, but more importantly in those small, splendid efforts that make headlines in the neighborhood newspaper instead of the national journal.

With these, we can build a great cathedral of the spirit—each of us raising it one stone at a time, as he reaches out to his neighbor, helping, caring, doing.

I do not offer a life of uninspiring ease. I do not call for a life of grim sacrifice. I ask you to join in a high adventure—one as rich as humanity itself, and exciting as the times we live in.

The essence of freedom is that each of us shares in the shaping of his own destiny.

Until he has been part of a cause larger than himself, no man is truly whole.

The way to fulfillment is in the use of our talents. We achieve nobility in the spirit that inspires that use.

As we measure what can be done, we shall promise only what we know we can produce; but as we chart our goals, we shall be lifted by our dreams.

No man can be fully free while his neighbor is not. To go forward at all is to go forward together.

This means black and white together, as one nation, not two. The laws have caught up with our conscience. What remains is to give life to what is in the law: to insure at last that as all are born equal in dignity before God, all are born equal in dignity before man.

As we learn to go forward together at home, let us also seek to go forward together with all mankind.

Let us take as our goal: Where peace is unknown, make it welcome; where peace is fragile, make it strong; where peace is temporary, make it permanent.

After a period of confrontation, we are entering an era of negotiation.

Let all nations know that during this administration our lines of communication will be open.

We seek an open world—open to ideas, open to the exchange of goods and people—a world in which no people, great or small, will live in angry isolation.

We cannot expect to make everyone our friend, but we can try to make no one our enemy.

Those who would be our adversaries, we invite to a peaceful competition—not in conquering territory or extending dominion, but in enriching the life of man.

As we explore the reaches of space, let us go to the new worlds together—not as new worlds to be conquered, but as a new adventure to be shared.

With those who are willing to join, let us cooperate to reduce the burden of arms, to strengthen the structure of peace, to lift up the poor and the hungry.

But to all those who would be tempted by weakness, let us leave no doubt that we will be as strong as we need to be for as long as we need to be.

Over the past 20 years, since I first came to this Capital as a freshman Congressman, I have visited most of the nations of the world. I have come to know the leaders of the world and the great forces, the hatreds, the fears that divide the world.

I know that peace does not come through wishing for it—that there is no substitute for days and even years of patient and prolonged diplomacy. I also know the people of the world.

I have seen the hunger of a homeless child, the pain of a man wounded in battle, the grief of a mother who has lost her son. I know these have no ideology, no race.

I know America. I know the heart of America is good.

I speak from my own heart, and the heart of my country, the deep concern we have for those who suffer and those who sorrow.

I have taken an oath today in the presence of God and my countrymen to uphold and defend the Constitution of the United States. To that oath I now add this sacred commitment: I shall consecrate my Office, my energies, and all the wisdom I can summon to the cause of peace among nations.

Let this message be heard by strong and weak alike:

The peace we seek—the peace we seek to win—is not victory over any other people, but the peace that comes "with healing in its wings"; with compassion for those who have suffered; with understanding for those who have opposed us; with the opportunity for all the peoples of this earth to choose their own destiny.

Only a few short weeks ago we shared the glory of man's first sight of the world as God sees it, as a single sphere reflecting light in the darkness.

As the Apollo astronauts flew over the moon's gray surface on Christmas Eve, they spoke to us of the beauty of earth—and in that voice so clear across the lunar distance, we heard them invoke God's blessing on its goodness.

In that moment, their view from the moon moved poet Archibald MacLeish to write: "To see the earth as it truly is, small and blue and beautiful in that eternal silence where it floats, is to see ourselves as riders on the earth together, brothers on that bright loveliness in the eternal cold—brothers who know now they are truly brothers."

In that moment of surpassing technological triumph, men turned their thoughts toward home and humanity—seeing in that far perspective that man's destiny on earth is not divisible; telling us that however far we reach into the cosmos, our destiny lies not in the stars but on earth itself, in our own hands, in our own hearts.

We have endured a long night of the American spirit. But as our eyes catch the dimness of the first rays of dawn, let us not curse the remaining dark. Let us gather the light. . . .

18.

“The present welfare system has to be judged a colossal failure” (August 8, 1969)

Nixon’s first domestic address—delivered, belatedly, seven months into his presidency—included two major proposals. The first was traditionally conservative: a “revenue sharing” arrangement designed to reduce the power of the federal bureaucracy and give more leeway to states and municipalities to spend federal funds. But Nixon was a poor manager of Congress, a body he held in contempt, and was not able to pass it until 1972.

The second proposal, a “Family Assistance Program,” would have replaced America’s main programs of relief to the poor, Aid to Families with Dependent Children, Food Stamps, and Medicaid, with a universal grant program with a floor of $1,600 for a family of four—an effective guaranteed minimum income, though one artfully devised to incentivize work. Nixon initially loved it because it would eviscerate the welfare bureaucracy. Liberals excoriated it for being inadequate (even though the minimum grant would have been three times that given to AFDC recipients in the stingiest state, Mississippi). Conservatives thought the program rewarded indolence—though in this speech, Nixon carefully fudged the description to claim it *would not. Nixon eventually lost interest in pursuing the reform, noting he would get credit for caring about the poor whether the program passed or not.*

. . . Whether measured by the anguish of the poor themselves, or by the drastically mounting burden on the taxpayer, the present welfare system has to be judged a colossal failure.

Our States and cities find themselves sinking in a welfare quagmire, as caseloads increase, as costs escalate, and as the welfare system stagnates enterprise and perpetuates dependency.

What began on a small scale in the depression 30's has become a huge monster in the prosperous 60's. And the tragedy is not only that it is bringing States and cities to the brink of financial disaster, but also that it is failing to meet the elementary human, social, and financial needs of the poor.

It breaks up homes. It often penalizes work. It robs recipients of dignity. And it grows.

Benefit levels are grossly unequal—for a mother with three children, they range from an average of $263 a month in one State, down to an average of only $39 in another State. Now such an inequality as this is wrong; no child is "worth" more in one State than in another State. One result of this inequality is to lure thousands more into already overcrowded inner cities, as unprepared for city life as they are for city jobs.

The present system creates an incentive for desertion. In most States a family is denied welfare payments if a father is present—even though he is unable to support his family. Now, in practice, this is what often happens: A father is unable to find a job at all or one that will support his children. And so, to make the children eligible for welfare, he leaves home—and the children are denied the authority, the discipline, the love that come with having a father in the home. This is wrong.

The present system often makes it possible to receive more money on welfare than on a low-paying job. This creates an incentive not to work, and it also is unfair to the working poor. It is morally wrong for a family that is working to try to make ends meet to receive less than a family across the street on welfare. This has been bitterly resented by the man who works, and rightly so—the rewards are just the opposite of what they should be. Its effect is to draw people off payrolls and onto welfare rolls—just the opposite of what government should be doing. To put it bluntly and simply—any system which makes it more profitable for a man not to work than to work, or which encourages a man to desert his family rather than to stay with his family, is wrong and indefensible.

We cannot simply ignore the failures of welfare, or expect them to go away. In the past 8 years, 3 million more people have been added to the welfare rolls—and this in a period of low unemployment. If the present trend continues, another 4 million will join the welfare rolls by 1975. The financial cost will be crushing; and the human cost will be suffocating.

That is why tonight I, therefore, propose that we will abolish the present welfare system and that we adopt in its place a new family assistance system. Initially, this new system will cost more than welfare. But, unlike welfare, it is designed to correct the condition it deals with and, thus, to lessen the long-range burden and cost.

Under this plan, the so-called "adult categories" of aid—aid to the aged, the blind, the disabled—would be continued, and a national minimum standard for benefits would be set, with the Federal Government contributing to its cost and also sharing the cost of additional State payments above that amount.

But the program now called "Aid to Families with Dependent Children"—the program we all normally think of when we think of "welfare"—would be done away with completely. The new family assistance system I propose in its place rests essentially on these three principles: equality of treatment across the Nation, a work requirement, and a work incentive.

Its benefits would go to the working poor, as well as the nonworking; to families with dependent children headed by a father, as well as to those headed by a mother; and a basic Federal minimum would be provided, the same in every State.

What I am proposing is that the Federal Government build a foundation under the income of every American family with dependent children that cannot care for itself—and wherever in America that family may live.

For a family of four now on welfare, with no outside income, the basic Federal payment would be $1,600 a year. States could add to that amount and most States would add to it. In no case would anyone's present level of benefits be lowered. At the same time, this foundation would be one on which the family itself could build. Outside earnings would be encouraged, not discouraged. The new worker could keep the first $60 a month of outside earnings with no reduction in his benefits; and beyond that, his benefits would be reduced by only 50 cents for each dollar earned.

By the same token, a family head already employed at low wages could get a family assistance supplement; those who work would no longer be discriminated against. For example, a family of five in which the father earns $2,000 a year—which is the hard fact of life for many families in America today—would get family assistance payments of $1,260, so that they would have a total income of $3,260. A family of seven earning $3,000 a year would have its income raised to $4,360.

Thus, for the first time, the government would recognize that it has no less an obligation to the working poor than to the nonworking poor; and for the first time, benefits would be scaled in such a way that it would always pay to work.

With such incentives, most recipients who can work will want to work. This is part of the American character.

But what of the others—those who can work but choose not to? Well, the answer is very simple. Under this proposal, everyone who accepts benefits must also accept work or training provided suitable jobs are available either locally or at some distance if transportation is provided. The only exceptions would be those unable to work and mothers of preschool children.

Even mothers of preschool children, however, would have the opportunity to work, because I am also proposing along with this a major expansion of day-care centers to make it possible for mothers to take jobs by which they can support themselves and their children.

This national floor under incomes for working or dependent families is not a "guaranteed income." Under the guaranteed income proposal, everyone would be assured a minimum income, regardless of how much he was capable of earning, regardless of what his need was, regardless of whether or not he was willing to work.

Now, during the presidential campaign last year, I opposed such a plan. I oppose it now and I will continue to oppose it, and this is the reason: A guaranteed income would undermine the incentive to work; the family assistance plan that I propose increases the incentive to work.

A guaranteed income establishes a right without any responsibilities; family assistance recognizes a need and establishes a responsibility. It provides help to those in need and, in turn, requires that those who receive help work to the extent of their capabilities. There is no reason why one person should be taxed so that another can choose to live idly.

In States that now have benefit levels above the Federal floor, family assistance would help ease the State's financial burdens. But in 20 States—those in which poverty is most widespread—the new Federal floor would be above present average benefits and would mean a leap upward for many thousands of families that cannot care for themselves. . . .

19.

"The great silent majority of my fellow Americans" (November 3, 1969)

Nixon's most famous speech from his first term was, on the one hand, a relatively complex and nuanced assessment of the strategic situation in Vietnam, a history lesson (if a misleading one), and the introduction of a new doctrine, "Vietnamization"—the eventual withdrawal of U.S. forces, alongside a demand for South Vietnam to defend itself. On the other it was a scurrilous slandering of those Americans who had been begging for exactly that. He said that antiwar protesters—two million had joined nationwide demonstrations two weeks earlier—wanted America to "lose in Vietnam." They invited "defeat and humiliation." Nixon, even as he announced slow retreat in a war he already knew to be a failure, asked for the support instead of that "great silent majority" who understood that "North Vietnam cannot defeat or humiliate the United States. Only Americans can do that."

The misdirection proved remarkably successful. Before the speech, 58 percent approved of his handling of the war. Afterward, 77 percent did.

Good evening, my fellow Americans:

Tonight I want to talk to you on a subject of

deep concern to all Americans and to many people in all parts of the world—the war in Vietnam.

I believe that one of the reasons for the deep division about Vietnam is that many Americans have lost confidence in what their Government has told them about our policy. The American people cannot and should not be asked to support a policy which involves the overriding issues of war and peace unless they know the truth about that policy.

Tonight, therefore, I would like to answer some of the questions that I know are on the minds of many of you listening to me.

How and why did America get involved in Vietnam in the first place?

How has this administration changed the policy of the previous administration?

What has really happened in the negotiations in Paris and on the battlefront in Vietnam?

What choices do we have if we are to end the war?

What are the prospects for peace? Now, let me begin by describing the situation I found when I was inaugurated on January 20.

—The war had been going on for 4 years.

—31,000 Americans had been killed in action.

—The training program for the South Vietnamese was behind schedule.

—540,000 Americans were in Vietnam with no plans to reduce the number.

—No progress had been made at the negotiations in Paris and the United States had not put forth a comprehensive peace proposal.

—The war was causing deep division at home and criticism from many of our friends as well as our enemies abroad.

In view of these circumstances there were some who urged that I end the war at once by ordering the immediate withdrawal of all American forces.

From a political standpoint this would have been a popular and easy course to follow. After all, we became involved in the war while my predecessor was in office. I could blame the defeat which would be the result of my action on him and come out as the peacemaker. Some put it to me quite bluntly: This was the only way to avoid allowing Johnson's war to become Nixon's war.

But I had a greater obligation than to think only of the years of my administration and of the next election. I had to think of the effect of my decision on the next generation and on the future of peace and freedom in America and in the world.

Let us all understand that the question before us is not whether some Americans are for peace and some Americans are against peace. The question at issue is not whether Johnson's war becomes Nixon's war.

The great question is: How can we win America's peace?

Well, let us turn now to the fundamental issue. Why and how did the United States become involved in Vietnam in the first place?

Fifteen years ago North Vietnam, with the logistical support of Communist China and the Soviet Union, launched a campaign to impose a Communist government on South Vietnam by instigating and supporting a revolution.

In response to the request of the Government of South Vietnam, President Eisenhower sent economic aid and military equipment to assist the people of South Vietnam in their efforts to prevent a Communist takeover. Seven years ago, President Kennedy sent 16,000 military personnel to Vietnam as combat advisers. Four years ago, President Johnson sent American combat forces to South Vietnam.

Now, many believe that President Johnson's decision to send American combat forces to South Vietnam was wrong. And many others—I among them—have been strongly critical of the way the war has been conducted.

But the question facing us today is: Now that we are in the war, what is the best way to end it?

In January I could only conclude that the precipitate withdrawal of American forces from Vietnam would be a disaster not only for South Vietnam but for the United States and for the cause of peace.

For the South Vietnamese, our precipitate withdrawal would inevitably allow the Communists to repeat the massacres which followed their takeover in the North 15 years before.

—They then murdered more than 50,000 people and hundreds of thousands more died in slave labor camps.

—We saw a prelude of what would happen in South Vietnam when the Communists entered the city of Hue last year. During their brief rule there, there was a bloody reign of terror in which 3,000 civilians were clubbed, shot to death, and buried in mass graves.

—With the sudden collapse of our support, these atrocities of Hue would become the nightmare of the entire nation—and particularly for the million and a half Catholic refugees who fled to South Vietnam when the Communists took over in the North. For the United States, this first defeat in our Nation's history would result in a collapse of confidence in American leadership, not only in Asia but throughout the world.

Three American Presidents have recognized the great stakes involved in Vietnam and understood what had to be done.

In 1963, President Kennedy, with his characteristic eloquence and clarity, said: "we want to see a stable government there, carrying on a struggle to maintain its national independence.

"We believe strongly in that. We are not going to withdraw from that effort. In my opinion, for us to withdraw from that effort would mean a collapse not only of South Viet-Nam, but Southeast Asia. So we are going to stay there."

President Eisenhower and President Johnson expressed the same conclusion during their terms of office.

For the future of peace, precipitate withdrawal would thus be a disaster of immense magnitude.

—A nation cannot remain great if it betrays its allies and lets down its friends.

—Our defeat and humiliation in South Vietnam without question would promote recklessness in the councils of those great powers who have not yet abandoned their goals of world conquest.

—This would spark violence wherever our commitments help maintain the peace—in the Middle East, in Berlin, eventually even in the Western Hemisphere.

Ultimately, this would cost more lives. It would not bring peace; it would bring more war.

For these reasons, I rejected the recommendation that I should end the war by immediately withdrawing all of our forces. I chose instead to change American policy on both the negotiating front and battlefront.

In order to end a war fought on many fronts, I initiated a pursuit for peace on many fronts.

In a television speech on May 14, in a speech before the United Nations, and on a number of other occasions I set forth our peace proposals in great detail.

—We have offered the complete withdrawal of all outside forces within 1 year.

—We have proposed a cease-fire under international supervision.

—We have offered free elections under international supervision with the Communists participating in the organization and conduct of the elections as an organized political force. And the Saigon Government has pledged to accept the result of the elections.

We have not put forth our proposals on a take-it-or-leave-it basis. We have indicated that we are willing to discuss the proposals that have been put forth by the other side. We have declared that anything is negotiable except the fight of the people of South Vietnam to determine their own future. At the Paris peace conference, Ambassador Lodge has demonstrated our flexibility and good faith in 40 public meetings.

Hanoi has refused even to discuss our proposals. They demand our unconditional acceptance of their terms, which are that we withdraw all American forces immediately and unconditionally and that we overthrow the Government of South Vietnam as we leave.

We have not limited our peace initiatives to public forums and public statements. I recognized, in January, that a long and bitter war like this usually cannot be settled in a public forum. That is why in addition to the public statements and negotiations I have explored every possible private avenue that might lead to a settlement.

Tonight I am taking the unprecedented step of disclosing to you some of our other initiatives for peace—initiatives we undertook privately and secretly because we thought we thereby might open a door which publicly would be closed.

I did not wait for my inauguration to begin my quest for peace.

—Soon after my election, through an individual who is directly in contact on a personal basis with the leaders of North Vietnam, I made two private offers for a rapid, comprehensive settlement. Hanoi's replies called in effect for our surrender before negotiations.

—Since the Soviet Union furnishes most of the military equipment for North Vietnam, Secretary of State Rogers, my Assistant for National Security Affairs, Dr. Kissinger, Ambassador Lodge, and I, personally, have met on a number of occasions with representatives of the Soviet Government to enlist their assistance in getting meaningful negotiations started. In addition, we have had extended discussions directed toward that same end with representatives of other governments which have diplomatic relations with North Vietnam. None of these initiatives have to date produced results.

—In mid-July, I became convinced that it was necessary to make a major move to break the deadlock in the Paris talks. I spoke directly in this office, where I am now sitting, with an individual who had known Ho Chi Minh [President, Democratic Republic of Vietnam] on a personal basis for 25 years. Through him I sent a letter to Ho Chi Minh. I did this outside of the usual diplomatic channels with the hope that with the necessity of making statements for propaganda removed, there might be constructive progress toward bringing the war to an end. Let me read from that letter to you now.

"Dear Mr. President:

"I realize that it is difficult to communicate meaningfully across the gulf of four years of war. But precisely because of this gulf, I wanted to take this opportunity to reaffirm in all solemnity my desire to work for a just peace. I deeply believe that the war in Vietnam has gone on too long and delay in bringing it to an end can benefit no one—least of all the people of Vietnam. . . .

"The time has come to move forward at the conference table toward an early resolution of this tragic war. You will find us forthcoming and open-minded in a common effort to bring the blessings of peace to the brave people of Vietnam. Let history record that at this critical juncture, both sides turned their face toward peace rather than toward conflict and war."

I received Ho Chi Minh's reply on August 30, 3 days before his death. It simply reiterated the public position North Vietnam had taken at Paris and flatly rejected my initiative.

The full text of both letters is being released to the press.

—In addition to the public meetings that I have referred to, Ambassador Lodge has met with Vietnam's chief negotiator in Paris in 11 private sessions.

—We have taken other significant initiatives which must remain secret to keep open some channels of communication which may still prove to be productive. But the effect of all the public, private, and secret negotiations which have been undertaken since the bombing halt a year ago and since this administration came into office on January 20, can be summed up in one sentence: No progress whatever has been made except agreement on the shape of the bargaining table. Well now, who is at fault?

It has become clear that the obstacle in negotiating an end to the war is not the President of the United States. It is not the South Vietnamese Government.

The obstacle is the other side's absolute refusal to show the least willingness to join us in seeking a just peace. And it will not do so while it is convinced that all it has to do is to wait for our next concession, and our next concession after that one, until it gets everything it wants.

There can now be no longer any question that progress in negotiation depends only on Hanoi's deciding to negotiate, to negotiate seriously.

I realize that this report on our efforts on the diplomatic front is discouraging to the American people, but the American people are entitled to know the truth—the bad news as well as the good news—where the lives of our young men are involved.

Now let me turn, however, to a more encouraging report on another front.

At the time we launched our search for peace I recognized we might not succeed in bringing an end to the war through negotiation. I, therefore, put into effect another plan to bring peace—a plan which will bring the war to an end regardless of what happens on the negotiating front.

It is in line with a major shift in U.S. foreign policy which I described in my press conference at Guam on July 25. Let me briefly explain what has been described as the Nixon Doctrine—a policy which not only will help end the war in Vietnam, but which is an essential element of our program to prevent future Vietnams.

We Americans are a do-it-yourself people. We are an impatient people. Instead of teaching someone else to do a job, we like to do it ourselves.

And this trait has been carried over into our foreign policy.

In Korea and again in Vietnam, the United States furnished most of the money, most of the arms, and most of the men to help the people of those countries defend their freedom against Communist aggression.

Before any American troops were committed to Vietnam, a leader of another Asian country expressed this opinion to me when I was traveling in Asia as a private citizen. He said: "When you are trying to assist another nation defend its freedom, U.S. policy should be to help them fight the war but not to fight the war for them."

Well, in accordance with this wise counsel, I laid down in Guam three principles as guidelines for future American policy toward Asia:

—First, the United States will keep all of its treaty commitments.

—Second, we shall provide a shield if a nuclear power threatens the freedom of a nation allied with us or of a nation whose survival we consider vital to our security.

—Third, in cases involving other types of aggression, we shall furnish military and economic assistance when requested in accordance with our treaty commitments. But we shall look to the nation directly threatened to assume the primary responsibility of providing the manpower for its defense.

After I announced this policy, I found that the leaders of the Philippines, Thailand, Vietnam, South Korea, and other nations which might be threatened by Communist aggression, welcomed this new direction in American foreign policy.

The defense of freedom is everybody's business—not just America's business. And it is particularly the responsibility of the people whose freedom is threatened. In the previous administration, we Americanized the war in Vietnam. In this administration, we are Vietnamizing the search for peace.

The policy of the previous administration not only resulted in our assuming the primary responsibility for fighting the war, but even more significantly did not adequately stress the goal of strengthening the South Vietnamese so that they could defend themselves when we left.

The Vietnamization plan was launched following Secretary Laird's visit to Vietnam in March. Under the plan, I ordered first a substantial increase in the training and equipment of South Vietnamese forces.

In July, on my visit to Vietnam, I changed General Abrams' orders so that they were consistent with the objectives of our new policies. Under the new orders, the primary mission of our troops is to enable the South Vietnamese forces to assume the full responsibility for the security of South Vietnam.

Our air operations have been reduced by over 20 percent.

And now we have begun to see the results of this long overdue change in American policy in Vietnam.

—After 5 years of Americans going into Vietnam, we are finally bringing American men home. By December 15, over 60,000 men will have been withdrawn from South Vietnam including 20 percent of all of our combat forces.

—The South Vietnamese have continued to gain in strength. As a result they have been able to take over combat responsibilities from our American troops.

Two other significant developments have occurred since this administration took office.

—Enemy infiltration, infiltration which is essential if they are to launch a major attack, over the last 3 months is less than 20 percent of what it was over the same period last year.

—Most important—United States casualties have declined during the last 2 months to the lowest point in 3 years.

Let me now turn to our program for the future.

We have adopted a plan which we have worked out in cooperation with the South Vietnamese for the complete withdrawal of all U.S. combat ground forces, and their replacement by South Vietnamese forces on an orderly scheduled timetable. This withdrawal will be made from strength and not from weakness. As South Vietnamese forces become stronger, the rate of American withdrawal can become greater.

I have not and do not intend to announce the timetable for our program. And there are obvious reasons for this decision which I am sure you will understand. As I have indicated on several occasions, the rate of withdrawal will depend on developments on three fronts.

One of these is the progress which can be or might be made in the Paris talks. An announcement of a fixed timetable for our withdrawal would completely remove any incentive for the enemy to negotiate an agreement. They would simply wait until our forces had withdrawn and then move in.

The other two factors on which we will base our withdrawal decisions are the level of enemy activity and the progress of the training programs of the South Vietnamese forces. And I am glad to be able to report tonight progress on both of these fronts has been greater than we anticipated when we started the program in June for withdrawal. As a result, our timetable for withdrawal is more optimistic now than when we made our first estimates in June. Now, this clearly demonstrates why it is not wise to be frozen in on a fixed timetable.

We must retain the flexibility to base each withdrawal decision on the situation as it is at that time rather than on estimates that are no longer valid.

Along with this optimistic estimate, I must—in all candor—leave one note of caution.

If the level of enemy activity significantly increases we might have to adjust our timetable accordingly.

However, I want the record to be completely clear on one point.

At the time of the bombing halt just a year ago, there was some confusion as to whether there was an understanding on the part of the enemy that if we stopped the bombing of North Vietnam they would stop the shelling of cities in South Vietnam. I want to be sure that there is no misunderstanding on the part of the enemy with regard to our withdrawal program.

We have noted the reduced level of infiltration, the reduction of our casualties, and are basing our withdrawal decisions partially on those factors.

If the level of infiltration or our casualties increase while we are trying to scale down the fighting, it will be the result of a conscious decision by the enemy.

Hanoi could make no greater mistake than to assume that an increase in violence will be to its advantage. If I conclude that increased enemy action jeopardizes our remaining forces in Vietnam, I shall not hesitate to take strong and effective measures to deal with that situation.

This is not a threat. This is a statement of policy, which as Commander in Chief of our Armed

Forces, I am making in meeting my responsibility for the protection of American fighting men wherever they may be.

My fellow Americans, I am sure you can recognize from what I have said that we really only have two choices open to us if we want to end this war.

—I can order an immediate, precipitate withdrawal of all Americans from Vietnam without regard to the effects of that action.

—Or we can persist in our search for a just peace through a negotiated settlement if possible, or through continued implementation of our plan for Vietnamization if necessary—a plan in which we will withdraw all of our forces from Vietnam on a schedule in accordance with our program, as the South Vietnamese become strong enough to defend their own freedom. I have chosen this second course. It is not the easy way. It is the right way.

It is a plan which will end the war and serve the cause of peace—not just in Vietnam but in the Pacific and in the world.

In speaking of the consequences of a precipitate withdrawal, I mentioned that our allies would lose confidence in America.

Far more dangerous, we would lose confidence in ourselves. Oh, the immediate reaction would be a sense of relief that our men were coming home. But as we saw the consequences of what we had done, inevitable remorse and divisive recrimination would scar our spirit as a people.

We have faced other crises in our history and have become stronger by rejecting the easy way out and taking the right way in meeting our challenges. Our greatness as a nation has been our capacity to do what had to be done when we knew our course was right.

I recognize that some of my fellow citizens disagree with the plan for peace I have chosen. Honest and patriotic Americans have reached different conclusions as to how peace should be achieved.

In San Francisco a few weeks ago, I saw demonstrators carrying signs reading: "Lose in Vietnam, bring the boys home."

Well, one of the strengths of our free society is that any American has a right to reach that conclusion and to advocate that point of view. But as President of the United States, I would be untrue to my oath of office if I allowed the policy of this Nation to be dictated by the minority who hold that point of view and who try to impose it on the Nation by mounting demonstrations in the street.

For almost 200 years, the policy of this Nation has been made under our Constitution by those leaders in the Congress and the White House elected by all of the people. If a vocal minority, however fervent its cause, prevails over reason and the will of the majority, this Nation has no future as a free society.

And now I would like to address a word, if I may, to the young people of this Nation who are particularly concerned, and I understand why they are concerned, about this war.

I respect your idealism.

I share your concern for peace. I want peace as much as you do. There are powerful personal reasons I want to end this war. This week I will have to sign 83 letters to mothers, fathers, wives, and loved ones of men who have given their lives for America in Vietnam. It is very little satisfaction to me that this is only one-third as many letters as I signed the first week in office. There is nothing I want more than to see the day come when I do not have to write any of those letters.

—I want to end the war to save the lives of those brave young men in Vietnam.

—But I want to end it in a way which will increase the chance that their younger brothers and their sons will not have to fight in some future Vietnam someplace in the world.

—And I want to end the war for another reason. I want to end it so that the energy and dedication of you, our young people, now too often directed into bitter hatred against those responsible for the war, can be turned to the great challenges of peace, a better life for all Americans, a better life for all people on this earth.

I have chosen a plan for peace. I believe it will succeed.

If it does succeed, what the critics say now won't matter. If it does not succeed, anything I say then won't matter.

I know it may not be fashionable to speak of patriotism or national destiny these days. But I feel it is appropriate to do so on this occasion.

Two hundred years ago this nation was weak and poor. But even then, America was the hope of millions in the world. Today we have become the strongest and richest nation in the world. And the wheel of destiny has turned so that any hope the world has for the survival of peace and freedom will be determined by whether the American people have the moral stamina and the courage to meet the challenge of free world leadership.

Let historians not record that when America was the most powerful nation in the world we passed on the other side of the road and allowed the last hopes for peace and freedom of millions of people to be suffocated by the forces of totalitarianism.

And so tonight—to you, the great silent majority of my fellow Americans—I ask for your support.

I pledged in my campaign for the Presidency to end the war in a way that we could win the peace. I have initiated a plan of action which will enable me to keep that pledge.

The more support I can have from the American people, the sooner that pledge can be redeemed; for the more divided we are at home, the less likely the enemy is to negotiate at Paris.

Let us be united for peace. Let us also be united against defeat. Because let us understand: North Vietnam cannot defeat or humiliate the United States. Only Americans can do that.

Fifty years ago, in this room and at this very desk, President Woodrow Wilson spoke words which caught the imagination of a war-weary world. He said: "This is the war to end war." His dream for peace after World War I was shattered on the hard realities of great power politics and Woodrow Wilson died a broken man.

Tonight I do not tell you that the war in Vietnam is the war to end wars. But I do say this: I have initiated a plan which will end this war in a way that will bring us closer to that great goal to which Woodrow Wilson and every American President in our history has been dedicated—the goal of a just and lasting peace.

As President I hold the responsibility for choosing the best path to that goal and then leading the Nation along it.

I pledge to you tonight that I shall meet this responsibility with all of the strength and wisdom I can command in accordance with your hopes, mindful of your concerns, sustained by your prayers.

Thank you and goodnight.

20.

"The postwar period in international relations has ended" ("State of the World" message, February 18, 1970)

When Nixon the politician needed to impress a potential supporter, he often unfurled a dazzling lecture wargaming the geopolitical situation across the globe. "One senses that he knows the political geography of planet earth about as well as most Congressmen know their own districts," one observer recalled. In his thirteenth month as president, Nixon delivered such a tour d'horizon for the benefit of the nation: the "First Annual Report to the Congress on United States Foreign Policy for the 1970s"—dubbed the "State of the World" message. The document's 37,425 words (printed in the next day's New York Times *as a stand-alone supplement) ranged across every corner of the globe and synthesized every strategic dilemma within the president's capacious field of vision. Compare its subtleties to the Manicheanism of his address on Alger Hiss, with its talk of "sinister conspiracy" and "the Red tide which to date has swept everything before it."*

The postwar period in international relations has ended.

Then, we were the only great power whose society and economy had escaped World War II's massive destruction. Today, the ravages of that war have been overcome. Western Europe and Japan have recovered their economic strength, their political vitality, and their national self-confidence. Once the recipients of American aid, they have now begun to share their growing resources with the developing world. Once almost totally dependent on American military power, our European allies now play a greater role in our common policies, commensurate with their growing strength.

Then, new nations were being born, often in turmoil and uncertainty. Today, these nations have a new spirit and a growing strength of independence. Once, many feared that they would become simply a battleground of cold-war rivalry and fertile ground for Communist penetration. But this fear misjudged their pride in their national identities and their determination to preserve their newly won sovereignty.

Then, we were confronted by a monolithic Communist world. Today, the nature of that world has changed—the power of individual Communist nations has grown, but international Communist unity has been shattered. Once a unified bloc, its solidarity has been broken by the powerful forces of nationalism. The Soviet Union and Communist China, once bound by an alliance of friendship, had become bitter adversaries by the mid-1960's. The only times the Soviet Union has used the Red Army since World War II have been against its own allies in East Germany in 1953, in Hungary in 1956, and in Czechoslovakia in 1968. The Marxist dream of international Communist unity has disintegrated.

Then, the United States had a monopoly or overwhelming superiority of nuclear weapons. Today, a revolution in the technology of war has altered the nature of the military balance of power. New types of weapons present new dangers. Communist China has acquired thermonuclear weapons. Both the Soviet Union and the United States have acquired the ability to inflict unacceptable damage on the other, no matter which strikes first. There can be no gain and certainly no victory for the power that provokes a thermonuclear exchange. Thus, both sides have recognized a vital mutual interest in halting the dangerous momentum of the nuclear arms race.

Then, the slogans formed in the past century were the ideological accessories of the intellectual debate. Today, the "isms" have lost their vitality—indeed the restlessness of youth on both sides of the dividing line testifies to the need for a new idealism and deeper purposes,

This is the challenge and the opportunity before America as it enters the 1970's. . . .

Few ideas have been so often or so loosely invoked as that of "Peace." But if peace is among the most overworked and often-abused staples of mankind's vocabulary, one of the reasons is that it is embedded so deeply in man's aspirations.

Skeptical and estranged, many of our young people today look out on a world they never made. They survey its conflicts with apprehension. Graduated into the impersonal routine of a bureaucratic, technological society, many of them see life as lonely conformity lacking the lift of a driving dream.

Yet there is no greater idealism, no higher adventure than taking a realistic road for peace. It is an adventure realized not in the exhilaration of a single moment, but in the lasting rewards of patient, detailed and specific efforts—a step at a time.

—Peace requires confidence—it needs the cement of trust among friends.

—Peace requires partnership—or else we will exhaust our resources, both physical and moral, in a futile effort to dominate our friends and forever isolate our enemies.—Peace must be just. It must answer man's dream of human dignity.

—Peace requires strength. It cannot be based on good will alone.

—Peace must be generous. No issue can be truly settled unless the solution brings mutual advantage.

—Peace must be shared. Other nations must feel that it is their peace just as we must feel that it is ours.

—And peace must be practical. It can only be found when nations resolve real issues, and accommodate each other's real interests. This requires not high rhetoric, but hard work.

These principles apply to our opponents as well as to our allies, to the less developed as well as the economically advanced nations. The peace we seek must be the work of all nations.

For peace will endure only when every nation has a greater stake in preserving than in breaking it.

I expressed these thoughts in my toast to the Acting President of India at New Delhi on July 31, 1969. I repeat it now:

"The concept of peace is as old as civilization, but the requirements of peace change with a changing world. Today we need a new definition of peace, one which recognizes not only the many threats to peace but also the many dimensions of peace.

"Peace is much more than the absence of war; and as Gandhi's life reminds us, peace is not the absence of change. Gandhi was a disciple of peace. He also was an architect of profound and far-reaching change. He stood for the achievement of change through peaceful methods, for belief in the power of conscience, for faith in the dignity and grace of the human spirit and in the rights of man.

"In today's rapidly changing world there is no such thing as a static peace or a stagnant order. To stand still is to build pressures that are bound to explode the peace; and more fundamentally, to stand still is to deny the universal aspirations of mankind. Peace today must be a creative force, a dynamic process, that embraces both the satisfaction of man's material needs and the fulfillment of his spiritual needs.

"The pursuit of peace means building a structure of stability within which the rights of each nation are respected: the rights of national independence, of self-determination, the right to be secure within its own borders and to be free from intimidation.

"This structure of stability can take many forms. Some may choose to join in formal alliances; some may choose to go their own independent way. We respect India's policy of nonalignment and its determination to play its role in the search for peace in its own way. What matters is not how peace is preserved, but that it be preserved; not the formal structure of treaties, but the informal network of common ideals and common purposes that together become a fabric of peace. What matters is not whether the principles of international behavior these represent are written or unwritten principles, but rather that they are accepted principles.

"Peace demands restraint. The truest peace expresses itself in self-restraint, in the voluntary acceptance, whether by men or by nations, of those basic rules of behavior that are rooted in mutual respect and demonstrated in mutual forbearance.

"When one nation claims the right to dictate the internal affairs of another, there is no peace.

"When nations arm for the purpose of threatening their weaker neighbors, there is no peace.

"There is true peace only when the weak are as safe as the strong, only when the poor can share the benefits of progress with the rich, and only when those who cherish freedom can exercise freedom.

"Gandhi touched something deep in the spirit of man. He forced the world to confront its conscience, and the world is better for having done so. Yet we still hear other cries, other appeals to our collective conscience as a community of man.

"The process of peace is one of answering those cries, yet doing so in a manner that preserves the right of each people to seek its own destiny in its own way and strengthens the principles of national sovereignty and national integrity, on which the structure of peace among nations depends.

"However fervently we believe in our own ideals, we cannot impose those ideals on others and still call ourselves men of peace. But we can assist others who share those ideals and who seek to give them life. As fellow members of the world community, we can assist the people of India in their heroic struggle to make the world's most populous democracy a model of orderly development and progress.

"There is a relationship between peace and freedom. Because man yearns for peace, when the people are free to choose their choice is more likely to be peace among nations; and because man yearns for freedom, when peace is secure the thrust of social evolution is toward greater freedom within nations.

"Essentially, peace is rooted in a sense of community: in a recognition of the common destiny of mankind, in a respect for the common dignity of mankind, and in the patterns of cooperation that make common enterprises possible. This is why the new patterns of regional cooperation emerging in Asia can be bulwarks of peace.

"In the final analysis, however, peace is a spiritual condition. All religions pray for it. Man must build it by reason and patience.

"On the moon, now, is a plaque bearing these simple words: 'We came in peace for all mankind.'

"Mahatma Gandhi came in peace to all mankind.

"In this spirit, then, let us all together commit ourselves to a new concept of peace:

—A concept that combines continuity and change, stability and progress, tradition and innovation;

—A peace that turns the wonders of science to the service of man;

—A peace that is both a condition and a process, a state of being and a pattern of change, a renunciation of war and a constructive alternative to revolution;

—A peace that values diversity and respects the right of different peoples to live by different systems—and freely to choose the systems they live by;

—A peace that rests on the determination of those who value it to preserve it but that looks forward to the reduction of arms and the ascendancy of reason;

—A peace responsive to the human spirit, respectful of the divinely inspired dignity of man, one that lifts the eyes of all to what man in brotherhood can accomplish and that now, as man crosses the threshold of the heavens, is more necessary than ever."

21.

Four Vietnam Statements (1970)

Richard Nixon regularly addressed the nation to inform the public of excellent progress in Vietnamization, each time announcing large numbers of troop reductions. One of the most dramatic came on April 20, 1970. His words that night gave the air of winding things down once and for all: "The decision I have announced tonight means that we finally have in sight the just peace we are seeking." Ten days later, on April 30, he shocked the nation by announcing that he was bringing the fight to a new nation, neutral Cambodia, where the enemy had established military sanctuaries. He undertook the action without consulting Congress, or indeed informing many of his foreign policy advisers. On college campuses, signs of militancy began flaring; on May 1 at Kent State University in Ohio three hundred students solemnly buried a copy of the Constitution. At the Pentagon, preceding a military briefing, Nixon held a hallway colloquy with admirers, one of whom told him that his speech the previous evening made her "proud to be an American." So Nixon gave an impromptu patriotic address in which he labeled campus protesters bums. (The White House released a transcript.) Campus uprisings escalated; at Kent State, students burned down the campus ROTC building. Na-

tional Guardsmen swarmed the campus and, on May 4, killed four unarmed student protesters in cold blood. Upwards of seven hundred universities suspended operations during the ensuing strikes, many for the rest of the school year.

("We finally have in sight the just peace we are seeking," April 20, 1970, Western White House, San Clemente, California)

Good evening, my fellow Americans:

I have requested this television and radio time tonight to give you a progress report on our plan to bring a just peace to Vietnam.

When I first outlined our program last June, I stated that the rate of American withdrawals from Vietnam would depend on three criteria: progress in the training and equipping of the South Vietnamese, progress in the Paris negotiations, and the level of enemy activity.

Tonight I am pleased to report that the progress in training and equipping South Vietnamese forces has substantially exceeded our original expectations last June.

Very significant advances have also been made in pacification.

Although we recognize that problems remain, these are encouraging trends.

However, I must report with regret that no progress has taken place on the negotiating front.

The enemy still demands that we unilaterally and unconditionally withdraw all American forces, that in the process we overthrow the elected Government of South Vietnam, and that the United States accept a political settlement that would have the practical consequences of the forcible imposition of a Communist government upon the people of South Vietnam.

That would mean humiliation and defeat for the United States. This we cannot and will not accept.

Let me turn to the third criterion for troop withdrawals—the level of enemy activity. In several areas last December, that level has substantially increased.

In recent months Hanoi has sent thousands more of their soldiers to launch new offensives in neutral Laos in violation of the Geneva Accords of 1969 to which they were signatories.

South of Laos, almost 40,000 Communist troops are now conducting overt aggression against Cambodia, a small neutralist country that the Communists have used for years as a base for attack upon South Vietnam in violation of the Geneva Accords to which they were also signatories. . . . However, despite this new enemy activity, there has been an overall decline in enemy force levels in South Vietnam since December. . . .

We have now reached a point where we can confidently move from a period of "cut and try" to a longer-range program for the replacement of Americans by South Vietnamese troops.

I am, therefore, tonight announcing plans for the withdrawal of an additional 150,000 American troops to be completed during the spring of next year. This will bring a total reduction of 265,000 men in our Armed Forces in Vietnam below the level that existed when we took office 15 months ago. . . .

I repeat what I said November 3 and December 15. If I conclude that increased enemy action jeopardizes our remaining forces in Vietnam, I shall not hesitate to take strong and effective measures to deal with that situation. . . .

The decision I have announced tonight means that we finally have in sight the just peace we are seeking. We can now say with confidence that pacification is succeeding. We can now say with confidence that the South Vietnamese can develop the capability for their own defense. And we can say with confidence that all American combat forces can and will be withdrawn. . . .

("A pitiful, helpless giant," April 30, 1970, the White House)

Good evening, my fellow Americans:

Ten days ago, in my report to the Nation on Vietnam, I announced a decision to withdraw an additional 150,000 Americans from Vietnam over the next year. I said then that I was making that decision despite our concern over increased enemy activity in Laos, in Cambodia, and in South Vietnam.

At that time, I warned that if I concluded that increased enemy activity in any of these areas endangered the lives of Americans remaining in Vietnam, I would not hesitate to take strong and effective measures to deal with that situation.

Despite that warning, North Vietnam has increased its military aggression in all these areas, and particularly in Cambodia.

After full consultation with the National Security Council, Ambassador Bunker, General Abrams, and my other advisors, I have concluded that the actions of the enemy in the last 10 days clearly endanger the lives of Americans who are in Vietnam now and would constitute an unacceptable risk to those who will be there after withdrawal of another 150,000.

To protect our men who are in Vietnam and to guarantee the continued success of our withdrawal and Vietnamization programs, I have concluded that the time has come for action. . . .

In cooperation with the armed forces of South Vietnam, attacks are being launched this week to clean out major enemy sanctuaries on the Cambodian-Vietnam border.

A major responsibility for the ground operations is being assumed by South Vietnamese forces. . . .

There is one area, however, immediately above Parrot's Beak, where I have concluded that a combined American and South Vietnamese operation is necessary.

Tonight, American and South Vietnamese units will attack the headquarters for the entire Communist military operation in South Vietnam. This key control center has been occupied by the North Vietnamese and Vietcong for 5 years in blatant violation of Cambodia's neutrality.

This is not an invasion of Cambodia. . . .

We take this action not for the purpose of expanding the war into Cambodia but for the purpose of ending the war in Vietnam and winning the just peace we all desire. . . .

The action that I have announced tonight puts the leaders of North Vietnam on notice that we will be patient in working for peace; we will be conciliatory at the conference table, but we will not be humiliated. We will not be defeated. We will not allow American men by the thousand to be killed by an enemy from privileged sanctuaries.

The time came long ago to end this war through peaceful negotiations. We stand ready for those negotiations. We have made major efforts, many of which must remain secret. I say tonight: All the offers and approaches made previously remain on the conference table whenever Hanoi is ready to negotiate seriously.

But if the enemy response to our most conciliatory offers for peaceful negotiations continues to be to increase its attacks and humiliate and defeat us, we shall react accordingly.

My fellow Americans, we live in an age of anarchy, both abroad and at home. We see mindless attacks on all the great institutions which have been created by free civilizations in the last 500 years. Even here in the United States, great universities are being systematically destroyed. Small nations all over the world find themselves under attack from within and from without.

If, when the chips are down, the world's most powerful nation, the United States of America, acts like a pitiful, helpless giant, the forces of totalitarianism and anarchy will threaten free nations throughout the world.

It is not our power but our will and character that is being tested tonight. . . .

("Those bums . . . blowing up the campuses," the Pentagon, May 1, 1970)

[*The day of Nixon's meeting with Pentagon officials on the Cambodian incursion, a Pentagon staffer congratulated him on the April 30 speech: "It made me proud to be an American."*]

Oh, how nice of you. . . . I wrote the speech. I finished it at 5 o'clock in the morning the night before. I had been writing for a little while. I had a lot of help from my staff, including people over here. Well, we could not do it without the backing of all of you, you know.

When it got down to the conclusion, then you say, well, the usual thing, you ask for support for the President and all that guff. Then you finally think of those kids out there. I say kids, I've seen them. They're the greatest.

You know, you see these bums, you know, blowing up the campuses. Listen, the boys on the college campuses today are the luckiest people in the world—going to the greatest universities—and here they are burning up the books, storming around about this issue, I mean—you name it. Get rid of the war and there'll be another one.

And then, out there, we got kids who are just doing their duty, and I've seen them: They stand tall and they're proud.

I'm sure they're scared. I was when I was there. But when it really comes down to it, they stand up and, boy, you've got to talk up for those men. They are going to do fine and we have to stand in back of them.

(White House statement on Kent State killings, May 4, 1970)

This should remind us all once again that when dissent turns to violence, it invites tragedy. It is my hope that this tragic and unfortunate incident will strengthen the determination of all the nation's campuses—administrations, faculty, and students alike—to stand firmly for the right which exists in this country of peaceful dissent and just as strongly against the resort to violence as a means of such expression.

22.

Two political statements (1970)

Richard Nixon considered ending the liberal hold on Congress in 1970 a life-and-death moment for his presidency. The White House undertook unprecedented efforts to tip the election in their favor. Instrumental to his plan was jump-starting the slow, unsteady process of recruiting conservative Southern voters to the Republican Party. He closed 1969 with a bid for their favor by nominating for the Supreme Court a South Carolinian, Clement Haynsworth, who was forced to withdraw because of financial improprieties; then a Georgian, G. Harrold Carswell, who quit under fire for his segregationist past and poor record as a judge. Nixon then went on TV to deliver a bitter speech claiming that Northern snobs would not let anyone with "the misfortune of being born in the South" serve on the nation's highest court.

The broader strategy In 1970 was to tie the breakdown in law and order to the Democrats. The point man was Vice President Spiro Agnew, who barnstormed the country saying things like, "To penetrate the cacophony of seditious drivel emanating from the best-publicized clowns in our society and their fans in the fourth estate, yes, my friends, to penetrate that drivel, we need a cry of alarm, not a whisper." The president joined him in October. A crucial part of the strategy was to allow in to campaign events small numbers of antiwar protesters who could be counted on to disrupt the proceedings; then Nixon would point them out for the news cameras and make them the subject of his speech.

The voters, however, overwhelmingly chose Democratic candidates, partly because of the poor economy, partly because Nixon seemed to be doing more to contribute to the nation's angry cacophony than to temper it (as he had seemed to be doing on the campaign trail in 1968). His ensuing frustration was a contributing factor in the stepped-up White House lawlessness that led to Watergate.

(White House TV speech on Supreme Court nominees, April 9, 1970)

I have reluctantly concluded—with the Senate as presently constituted—I cannot successfully nominate to the Supreme Court any Federal appellate judge from the South who believes as I do in the strict construction of the Constitution. Judges Carswell and Haynsworth have endured with admirable dignity vicious assaults on their intelligence, their honesty, and their character. They have been falsely charged with being racist. But when all the hypocrisy is stripped away, the real issue was their philosophy of strict construction of the Constitution, a philosophy that I share, and the fact that they had the misfortune of being born in the South. After the rejection of Judge Carswell and Judge Haynsworth, this conclusion is inescapable.

Both are distinguished jurists; both are among the finest judges in the Fourth and Fifth Circuits; both had previously been approved by the Senate for the second highest Federal court; yet, both were rejected. In my opinion, neither would have been rejected had he not been born in a Southern State.

In selecting both men, I had several criteria in mind. First and foremost, they had to be men who shared my legal philosophy of strict construction of the Constitution, men who would help to restore to the United States Supreme Court the balance that it genuinely needs—that balance I pledged to the American people that I would help to restore.

Secondly, I set the criteria that both have experience on the highest Federal appeals court—next to the United States Supreme Court itself.

Third, I chose them because they were both men of the South.

I do not believe that any segment of our people or any section of the country can lay claim to one or more seats on the High Court as its own preserve. But controversial and far-reaching decisions of past and coming years are far better received when each section of the country and every major segment of our people can look to the Court and see there its legal philosophy articulately represented.

Four of the present members of the Court are from the East, one from the Midwest, two from the West, and one from the South. More than one-fourth of the people of this Nation live in the South; they deserve representation on the Court.

But more important than geographical balance is philosophical balance—the need to have represented on the Court those who believe in strict construction of the Constitution as well as others who believe in the liberal construction which has constituted the majority on the Court for the past 15 years.

With yesterday's action, the Senate has said that no southern Federal appellate judge who believes in a strict interpretation of the Constitution can be elevated to the Supreme Court.

As long as the Senate is constituted the way it is today, I will not nominate another southerner and let him be subjected to the kind of malicious character assassination accorded both Judges Haynsworth and Carswell. However, my next nomination will be made in the very near future; a President should not leave that vacancy on the Court when it can be filled. My next nominee will be from outside the South and he will fulfill the criteria of a strict constructionist with judicial experience either from a Federal bench or on a State appeals court.

I understand the bitter feeling of millions of Americans who live in the South about the act of regional discrimination that took place in the Senate yesterday. They have my assurance that the day will come when men like Judges Carswell and Haynsworth can and will sit on the High Court.

("It's time for the great silent majority of this country to stand up and be counted," Grand Forks, South Dakota, October 19, 1970)

Yesterday, I called our neighbor to the north, the Prime Minister of Canada. I expressed my sympathy to him for what had happened there—you remember reading about it in the paper and hearing about it on the television—where a government official was kidnapped; the cause had something to do about the liberation of Quebec. That is not the important thing. But the government official was kidnapped; ransom and blackmail was demanded. The Prime Minister refused to pay it and the government official was killed.

That was a terrible tragedy. That didn't happen in some faraway country. It happened in Canada. And that also happens in the United States. All over this land we see a new doctrine developing in recent years, that if the cause is one you believe in, and if the cause is right, any means is right to serve that cause. You can bomb a building. You can burn a building. You can engage in illegal conduct. You can not only demonstrate peacefully, but you can shout four-letter obscenities in a crowd. You can do all these things and the cause justifies it.

And we also see a rising rate of terrorism and crime across this country. I have been trying to do something about it, but I need some help. I want to tell you why.

I submitted a crime control bill, the whole package, to the Congress 18 months ago. And only one of them, the only major one, the organized crime bill, came to my desk just a week ago. But the one that would stop the flow of obscenity and filth into the homes where children are living, that isn't there yet. The one that would allow me to deal with, as it must be dealt with, the dangerous traffic in narcotics and dangerous drugs, it still isn't on the President's desk. And there is something else, too.

If we are going to stop the rise in crime in this country, we not only have to have laws, we have to have judges in the courts of this land who will enforce the laws, and enforce them effectively and fairly.

My friends, the President of the United States can ask for the laws and the President of the United States can appoint judges. But the Senate of the United States has to approve those laws and it must approve those judges. And I know where

Tom Kleppe stands, not just in election, but all year round. He is strong for law and order and justice. And we need that kind of man in the United States Senate representing North Dakota.

Finally, I come to the key point that I think we all have to realize. I do appreciate the fact that in this audience there are those who disagree, those who agree. I appreciate your courtesy in listening to what I have had to say. We have had some rather interesting experiences in the last couple of days. They don't particularly bother me. After all, I have been heckled quite a bit during my political career, not just here but abroad as well. Saturday in Vermont, they threw a few rocks. In New Jersey, they shouted a bit. And so it was today earlier in Columbus, Ohio.

And so, the impression gets around the country, a false impression, that young Americans are all like that, that young Americans express their disagreement, not by courteously listening and then arguing their point of view, but that they always have to try to shout down a speaker, use four-letter obscenities, or even engage in violence.

And the reason that that is the impression across this country is that on our television screen night after night, you see it, you know, a building burned here, demonstrators shouting here, throwing rocks at the President there, or whatever the case might be.

Let me tell you something. I have news for you. That isn't a majority of young America. I have faith in young America, and I will tell you why. Because the majority of young Americans, they want progress for this country, they want peace for this country, they may not agree with every program that we have, but they also recognize that the way to progress and the way to peace is not through engaging in violence. And they also recognize that you are not going to learn anything unless you listen.

I simply want to say this: People will tell me; I have been asked, "What do you do? How do you answer those who throw rocks, shout their four-letter obscenities? Do you do it, do you answer in kind?" The answer is no, not at all. I will tell you what you do. You have got an answer. It is the most powerful answer in the world. It's time for the great silent majority of this country to stand up and be counted, and the way you can stand up and be counted is on election day. Go to the polls and vote.

Remember, the four-letter word that is most powerful of all the four letters in the world is vote—v-o-t-e.

23.

"Our best days lie ahead" (August 15, 1971)

As late as August 4, 1971, President Nixon repeated his conviction that the Democrats' preferred reform for inflation and recession, wage and price controls, "would stifle the American economy, its dynamism, its productivity, and would be . . . a mortal blow to the United States as a first-class economic power." Eleven days later, he instituted wage and price controls.

The president had decided that America's economic dominance in the world was indeed in decline, that there was little he could about it, and that one of the reasons he had to be reelected with an overwhelming mandate was that Nixon, and only Nixon, safely removed from the requirement of winning another election, could cushion the blow of teaching America to live within limits. The previous month, to a more esoteric audience—newspaper owners—he had all but admitted this. Now, however, to the TV public, he gave a jingoistic speech arguing that wage and price controls were the royal road to keeping America a first-class economic power, and blaming "international money speculators," and ungrateful foreign nations forcing "the United States to compete with one hand tied behind her back," for all America's economic woes. The reforms he announced were part of a number of strategies to artificially stimulate the economy in time for the 1972 elections.

Good evening:

I have addressed the Nation a number of times over the past years on the problems of ending a war. Because of the progress we have made toward achieving that goal, this Sunday evening is an appropriate time for us to turn our attention to the challenges of peace.

America today has the best opportunity in this century to achieve two of its greatest ideals: to bring about a full generation of peace, and to create a new prosperity without war.

This not only requires bold leadership ready to take bold action—it calls forth the greatness in a great people.

Prosperity without war requires action on three fronts: We must create more and better jobs; we must stop the rise in the cost of living; we must protect the dollar from the attacks of international money speculators. . . .

In the past 7 years, there has been an average of one international monetary crisis every year. Now who gains from these crises? Not the workingman; not the investor; not the real producers of wealth. The gainers are the international money speculators. Because they thrive on crises, they help to create them.

In recent weeks, the speculators have been waging an all-out war on the American dollar. The strength of a nation's currency is based on the strength of that nation's economy—and the American economy is by far the strongest in the world. Accordingly, I have directed the Secretary of the Treasury to take the action necessary to defend the dollar against the speculators.

I have directed Secretary Connally to suspend temporarily the convertibility of the dollar into gold or other reserve assets, except in amounts and conditions determined to be in the interest of monetary stability and in the best interests of the United States.

Now, what is this action—which is very technical—what does it mean for you?

Let me lay to rest the bugaboo of what is called devaluation.

If you want to buy a foreign car or take a trip abroad, market conditions may cause your dollar to buy slightly less. But if you are among the overwhelming majority of Americans who buy American-made products in America, your dollar will be worth just as much tomorrow as it is today.

The effect of this action, in other words, will be to stabilize the dollar.

Now, this action will not win us any friends among the international money traders. But our primary concern is with the American workers, and with fair competition around the world. . . .

As a result of these actions, the product of American labor will be more competitive, and the unfair edge that some of our foreign competition has will be removed. This is a major reason why our trade balance has eroded over the past 15 years.

At the end of World War II the economies of the major industrial nations of Europe and Asia were shattered. To help them get on their feet and to protect their freedom, the United States has provided over the past 25 years $143 billion in foreign aid. That was the right thing for us to do.

Today, largely with our help, they have regained their vitality. They have become our strong competitors, and we welcome their success. But now that other nations are economically strong, the time has come for them to bear their fair share of the burden of defending freedom around the world. The time has come for exchange rates to be set straight and for the major nations to compete as equals. There is no longer any need for the United States to compete with one hand tied behind her back. . . .

The purposes of the Government actions I have announced tonight are to lay the basis for renewed confidence, to make it possible for us to compete fairly with the rest of the world, to open the door to new prosperity.

But government, with all of its powers, does not hold the key to the success of a people. That key, my fellow Americans, is in your hands.

A nation, like a person, has to have a certain inner drive in order to succeed. In economic affairs, that inner drive is called the competitive spirit.

Every action I have taken tonight is designed to nurture and stimulate that competitive spirit, to help us snap out of the self-doubt, the self-disparagement that saps our energy and erodes our confidence in ourselves.

Whether this Nation stays number one in the world's economy or resigns itself to second, third, or fourth place; whether we as a people have faith in ourselves, or lose that faith; whether we hold fast to the strength that makes peace and freedom possible in this world, or lose our grip—all that depends on you, on your competitive spirit, your sense of personal destiny, your pride in your country and in yourself.

We can be certain of this: As the threat of war recedes, the challenge of peaceful competition in the world will greatly increase.

We welcome competition, because America is at her greatest when she is called on to compete.

As there always have been in our history, there will be voices urging us to shrink from that challenge of competition, to build a protective wall around ourselves, to crawl into a shell as the rest of the world moves ahead.

Two hundred years ago a man wrote in his diary these words: "Many thinking people believe America has seen its best days." That was written in 1775, just before the American Revolution—the dawn of the most exciting era in the history of man. And today we hear the echoes of those voices, preaching a gospel of gloom and defeat, saying the same thing: "We have seen our best days."

I say, let Americans reply: "Our best days lie ahead."

24.

"One China" (February 24, 1972)

Nixon and Chairman Mao Zedong's "serious and frank exchange of views on Sino-U.S. relations" was actually if anything less profound than the 1959 "Kitchen Debate" with Khrushchev; Mao was so old and frail Nixon almost didn't get to meet him. And Nixon's grand dream for his historic China trip—unleashing Chinese pressure to end the Vietnam War—was a fantasy. But the symbolism of the week-long summit was colossal. All three networks devoted four hours of live coverage to the opening banquet. The most important diplomatic result, negotiated over days-long marathon sessions—the State Department was left out of the proceedings—concerned Taiwan, which China claimed as part of its territory, but which America backed as an independent anti-Communist nation. The new status quo would be a strange, Kafka-esque "one China" policy—basically, an agreement to pretend the problem didn't exist.

The communiqué is ironic for what it nearly omits. There is only one tiny paragraph on trade. As Kissinger whispered to Nixon, "The maximum amount of bilateral trade possible between us, even if we make great efforts, is infinitesimal in terms of our total economy."

President Richard Nixon of the United States of America visited the People's Republic of China at the invitation of Premier Chou En-lai of the People's Republic of China from February 21 to February 28, 1972. Accompanying the President were Mrs. Nixon, U.S. Secretary of State William Rogers, Assistant to the President Dr. Henry Kissinger, and other American officials.

President Nixon met with Chairman Mao Tsetung of the Communist Party of China on February 21. The two leaders had a serious and frank exchange of views on Sino-U.S. relations and world affairs.

During the visit, extensive, earnest, and frank discussions were held between President Nixon and Premier Chou En-lai on the normalization of relations between the United States of America and the People's Republic of China, as well as on other matters of interest to both sides. In addition, Secretary of State William Rogers and Foreign Minister Chi P'engfei held talks in the same spirit.

President Nixon and his party visited Peking and viewed cultural, industrial and agricultural sites, and they also toured Hangchow and Shanghai where, continuing discussions with Chinese leaders, they viewed similar places of interest.

The leaders of the People's Republic of China and the United States of America found it beneficial to have this opportunity, after so many years without contact, to present candidly to one another their views on a variety of issues. They reviewed the international situation in which important changes and great upheavals are taking place and expounded their respective positions and attitudes.

The U.S. side stated: Peace in Asia and peace in the world requires efforts both to reduce immediate tensions and to eliminate the basic causes of conflict. The United States will work for a just and secure peace: just, because it fulfills the aspirations of peoples and nations for freedom and progress; secure, because it removes the danger of foreign aggression. The United States supports individual freedom and social progress for all the peoples of the world, free of outside pressure or intervention. The United States believes that the effort to reduce tensions is served by improving communication between countries that have different ideologies so as to lessen the risks of confrontation through accident, miscalculation or misunderstanding. Countries should treat each other with mutual respect and be willing to compete peacefully, letting performance be the ultimate judge. No country should claim infallibility and each country should be prepared to re-examine its own attitudes for the common good. The United States stressed that the peoples of Indochina should be allowed to determine their destiny without outside intervention; its constant primary objective has been a negotiated solution; the eight-point proposal put forward by the Republic of Vietnam and the United States on January 27, 1972 represents a basis for the attainment of that objective; in the absence of a negotiated settlement the United States envisages the ultimate withdrawal of all U.S. forces from the region consistent with the aim of self-determination for each country of Indochina. The United States will maintain its close ties with and support for the Republic of Korea; the United States will support efforts of the Republic of Korea to seek a relaxation of tension and increased communication in the Korean peninsula. The United States places the highest value on its friendly relations with Japan; it will continue to develop the existing close bonds. Consistent with the United Nations Security Council Resolution of December 21, 1971, the United States favors the continuation of the cease-fire between India and Pakistan and the withdrawal of all military forces to within their own territories and to their own sides of the cease-fire line in Jammu and Kashmir; the United States supports the right of the peoples of South Asia to shape their own future in peace, free of military threat, and without having the area become the subject of great power rivalry.

The Chinese side stated: Wherever there is oppression, there is resistance. Countries want independence, nations want liberation and the people want revolution—this has become the irresistible trend of history. All nations, big or small, should be equal; big nations should not bully the small and strong nations should not bully the weak. China will never be a superpower and it opposes hegemony and power politics of any kind. The Chinese side stated that it firmly supports the struggles of all the oppressed people and nations for freedom and liberation and that the people of all countries have the right to choose their social systems according to their own wishes and the right to safeguard the independence, sovereignty and territorial integrity of their own countries and oppose foreign aggression, interference, control and subversion. All foreign troops should be withdrawn to their own countries.

The Chinese side expressed its firm support to the peoples of Vietnam, Laos, and Cambodia in their efforts for the attainment of their goal and its firm support to the seven-point proposal of the Provisional Revolutionary Government of the Republic of South Vietnam and the elaboration of February this year on the two key problems in the proposal, and to the Joint Declaration of the Summit Conference of the Indo-Chinese Peoples. It firmly supports the eight-point program for the peaceful unification of Korea put forward by the Government of the Democratic People's Republic of Korea on April 12, 1971, and the stand for the abolition of the "U.N. Commission for the Unification and Rehabilitation of Korea." It firmly opposes the revival and outward expansion of Japanese militarism and firmly supports the Japanese people's desire to build an independent, democratic, peaceful and neutral Japan. It firmly maintains that India and Pakistan should, in accordance with the United Nations resolutions on the India-Pakistan question, immediately withdraw all their forces to their respective territories and to their own sides of the cease fire line in Jammu and Kashmir and firmly supports the Pakistan Government and people in their struggle to preserve their independence and sovereignty and the people of Jammu and Kashmir in their struggle for the right of self-determination.

There are essential differences between China and the United States in their social systems and foreign policies. However, the two sides agreed that countries, regardless of their social systems, should conduct their relations on the principles of respect for the sovereignty and territorial integrity of all states, nonaggression against other states, noninterference in the internal affairs of other states, equality and mutual benefit, and peaceful coexistence. International disputes should be settled on this basis, without resorting to the use or threat of force. The United States and the People's Republic of China are prepared to apply these principles to their mutual relations.

With these principles of international relations in mind the two sides stated that:

—progress toward the normalization of relations between China and the United States is in the interests of all countries;

—both wish to reduce the danger of international military conflict;

—neither should seek hegemony in the Asia-Pacific region and each is opposed to efforts by any other country or group of countries to establish such hegemony; and

—neither is prepared to negotiate on behalf of any third party or to enter into agreements or understandings with the other directed at other states.

Both sides are of the view that it would be against the interests of the peoples of the world for any major country to collude with another against other countries, or for major countries to divide up the world into spheres of interest.

The two sides reviewed the long-standing serious disputes between China and the United States. The Chinese side reaffirmed its position: The Taiwan question is the crucial question obstructing the normalization of relations between China and the United States; the Government of the People's Republic of China is the sole legal government of China; Taiwan is a province of China which has long been returned to the motherland; the liberation of Taiwan is China's internal affair in which no other country has the right to interfere; and all U.S. forces and military installations must be withdrawn from Taiwan. The Chinese Government firmly opposes any activities which aim at the creation of "one China, one Taiwan, . . . one China, two governments," "two Chinas," and "independent Taiwan" or advocate that "the status of Taiwan remains to be determined."

The U.S. side declared: The United States acknowledges that all Chinese on either side of the Taiwan Strait maintain there is but one China and that Taiwan is a part of China. The United States Government does not challenge that position. It reaffirms its interest in a peaceful settlement of the Taiwan question by the Chinese themselves. With this prospect in mind, it affirms the ultimate objective of the withdrawal of all U.S. forces and military installations from Taiwan. In the meantime, it will progressively reduce its forces and military installations on Taiwan as the tension in the area diminishes.

The two sides agreed that it is desirable to broaden the understanding between the two peoples. To this end, they discussed specific areas in such fields as science, technology, culture, sports and journalism, in which people-to-people contacts and exchanges would be mutually beneficial. Each side undertakes to facilitate the further development of such contacts and exchanges.

Both sides view bilateral trade as another area from which mutual benefit can be derived, and agreed that economic relations based on equality and mutual benefit are in the interest of the people of the two countries. They agree to facilitate the progressive development of trade between their two countries.

The two sides agreed that they will stay in contact through various channels, including the sending of a senior U.S. representative to Peking from time to time for concrete consultations to further the normalization of relations between the two countries and continue to exchange views on issues of common interest.

The two sides expressed the hope that the gains achieved during this visit would open up new prospects for the relations between the two countries. They believe that the normalization of relations between the two countries is not only in the interest of the Chinese and American peoples but also contributes to the relaxation of tension in Asia and the world.

President Nixon, Mrs. Nixon and the American party expressed their appreciation for the gracious hospitality shown them by the Government and people of the People's Republic of China.

25.

“He can undisappear if we want him to” (June 23, 1972)

The two men who coordinated the burglary of the Democratic National Committee headquarters from a Howard Johnson’s across the street, James McCord and Howard Hunt, were close associates of the Nixon reelection campaign and White House. Covering up those ties was the original task of the cover-up. Here, Nixon and chief of staff Bob Haldeman brainstorm a phony motive for the break-in to launder through the press. The burglars were Cuban, so blaming Cuban nationalists—who were always showing up in the news committing crimes against supposed allies and enablers of Fidel Castro—was one possibility. They note how the White House taping system “complicates things”—i.e., provides an evidentiary record of their ongoing obstruction of justice. Then when they realize that documentary evidence limits their ability to isolate their crimes from the White House, Nixon, frustrated, rehearses a line to distract the media: “the committee isn’t worth bugging.”

Later, they arrive at an apparently foolproof plan. FBI investigators were on the verge of cracking the case, to Nixon’s dismay. Howard Hunt was a former CIA operative who helped lead the attempt to over-

throw Castro at the Bay of Pigs in Cuba in 1961. FBI director Pat Gray could be ordered to end the investigation on the pretext that it might jeopardize national security by compromising CIA secrets.

Mark Felt, the FBI's number two officer, also mentioned in the conversation, would later serve as Washington Post *reporters Bob Woodward and Carl Bernstein's secret source, "Deep Throat," on the White House's crimes.*

HALDEMAN: McCord, I guess, will say that he was working with the Cubans, he wanted to put this in for their own political reasons. But Hunt disappeared or is in the process of disappearing. He can undisappear if we want him to. He can disappear to a Latin American country. But at least the original thought was that that would do it, that he might want to disappear, [unintelligible] on the basis that these guys, the Cubans—see, he was in the Bay of Pigs thing. One of the Cubans, Barker, the guy with the American name, was his deputy in the Bay of Pigs operation and so they're kind of trying to tie it to the Cuban nationalists.

NIXON: We are?

HALDEMAN: Yes. Now of course they're trying to tie these guys to Colson, the White House. It's strange—if Colson doesn't run out, it doesn't go anywhere. The closest they come he [Hunt] was a consultant to Colson. We have detailed somewhat the nature of his consulting fee and said it was basically [unintelligible]. I don't know.

NIXON: You don't know what he did?

HALDEMAN: I think we all knew that there were some—

NIXON: Intelligence.

HALDEMAN: Some activities, and we were getting reports, or some input anyway. But I don't think—I don't think Chuck knew specifically that this was under way. He seems to take all the blame himself.

NIXON: Did he? Good.

This Oval Office business complicates things all over.

HALDEMAN: They say it's extremely good. I haven't listened to the tapes.

NIXON: They're kept for future purposes. . . .

HALDEMAN: Nobody monitors those tapes, obviously. They are kept stacked up and locked up in a super-secure—there are only three people that know. If they get all the circumstantial stuff tied together, maybe it's better . . . to plead guilty, saying we were spying on the Democrats. Just let the Cubans say, we, McCord . . . figured it was safe for us to use.

NIXON: Well, they've got to plead guilty.

HALDEMAN: And we went in there to get this because we're scared to death that this crazy man's going to become President and sell the U.S. out to the Communists.

NIXON: Now was he [Hunt] directly involved?

HALDEMAN: He was across the street in the Howard Johnson Motel with a direct line of sight room, observing across the street. And that was the room in which they have the receiving equipment for the bugs.

NIXON: Well, does Hunt work for us or what?

HALDEMAN: No. Oh, we don't know. I don't know. I don't know if that's one—that's something I haven't gotten an answer to, how—apparently McCord had Hunt working with him, or Hunt had McCord working with him, and with these Cubans. They're all tied together. Hunt when he ran the Bay of Pigs thing was working with this guy Barker, one of the Cubans who was arrested.

NIXON: How does the press know about this?

HALDEMAN: They don't. Oh, they know Hunt's involved because they found his name in the address book of two of the Cubans, Barker's book and one of the other guy's books. He's identified as "White House." And also because one of the Cubans had a check from Hunt, a check for $690 or something like that, which Hunt had given to this Cuban to take back to Miami with him and mail. It was to pay his country club bill.

NIXON: Hunt?

HALDEMAN: Hunt, yes. Probably so he can pay nonresident dues at the country club or something. But anyway, they had that check, so that was another tie.

NIXON: Well, in a sense, if the Cubans—the fact that Hunt's involved with the Cubans or McCord's involved with the Cubans, here are the Cuban people. . . . My God, the committee isn't worth bugging in my opinion, that's my public line. . . .

HALDEMAN: . . . the way to handle this now is for us to have Walters call Pat Gray and just say, "Stay the hell out of this . . . this is ah, business here we don't want you to go any further on it." That's not an unusual development. . . .

NIXON: Um huh.

HALDEMAN: . . . and, uh, that would take care of it.

NIXON: What about Pat Gray, ah, you mean he doesn't want to?

HALDEMAN: Pat does want to. He doesn't know how to, and he doesn't have, he doesn't have any basis for doing it. Given this, he will then have the basis. He'll call Mark Felt in, and the two of them . . . and Mark Felt wants to cooperate because. . . .

NIXON: Yeah.

HALDEMAN: He's ambitious. . . .

NIXON: Yeah.

HALDEMAN: Ah, he'll call him in and say, "We've got the signal from across the river to, to put the hold on this." And that will fit rather well because the FBI agents who are working the case, at this point, feel that's what it is. This is CIA. . . .

NIXON: When you get in these people when you . . . get these people in, say: "Look, the problem is that this will open the whole, the whole Bay of Pigs thing, and the President just feels that" ah, without going into the details . . . don't, don't lie to them to the extent to say there is no involvement, but just say this is sort of a comedy of errors, bizarre, without getting into it, "the President believes that it is going to open the whole Bay of Pigs thing up again. And, ah, because these people are plugging for, for keeps and that they should call the FBI in and say that we wish for the country, don't go any further into this case," period!

HALDEMAN: OK.

NIXON: That's the way to put it, do it straight [unintelligible]. . . .

26.

"Her name was Tanya" (August 23, 1972)

Richard Nixon campaigned for president in 1972 by practically not campaigning at all. As surrogate speakers and TV commercials sponsored by "Democrats for Nixon" made the argument that the Democrats had veered dangerously from the American mainstream, Nixon emphasized his role as commander in chief, the peacemaker who had reached out to China, and in May inked a disarmament deal in Moscow. At the Republican convention in Miami Beach, a BBC reporter discovered a literal script specifying the exact timing for "spontaneous" applause and "impromptu" remarks. Richard Nixon frequently ended his speeches with sentimental stories about children; in his 1972 acceptance, his voice broke as he told the story of Tanya, a little Russian girl who was the only person in her family to survive World War II. Peace for all the world's children was the meaning, he said, of his presidency. He won reelection with 49 of 50 states in his column, the Watergate story barely surfacing in polls as a concern of the public at all.

My fellow Americans, we stand today on the threshold of one of the most exciting and challenging eras in the history of relations between nations.

We have the opportunity in our time to be the peacemakers of the world, because the world trusts and respects us and because the world knows that we shall only use our power to defend freedom, never to destroy it; to keep the peace, never to break it.

A strong America is not the enemy of peace; it is the guardian of peace.

The initiatives that we have begun can result in reducing the danger of arms, as well as the danger of war which hangs over the world today.

Even more important, it means that the enormous creative energies of the Russian people and the Chinese people and the American people and all the great peoples of the world can be turned away from production of war and turned toward production for peace.

In America it means that we can undertake programs for progress at home that will be just as exciting as the great initiatives we have undertaken in building a new structure of peace abroad.

My fellow Americans, the peace dividend that we hear so much about has too often been described solely in monetary terms—how much money we could take out of the arms budget and apply to our domestic needs. By far the biggest dividend, however, is that achieving our goal of a lasting peace in the world would reflect the deepest hopes and ideals of all of the American people.

Speaking on behalf of the American people, I was proud to be able to say in my television address to the Russian people in May: We covet no one else's territory. We seek no dominion over any other nation. We seek peace not only for ourselves, but for all the people of the world.

This dedication to idealism runs through America's history.

During the tragic War Between the States, Abraham Lincoln was asked whether God was on his side. He replied, "My concern is not whether God is on our side, but whether we are on God's side."

May that always be our prayer for America.

We hold the future of peace in the world and our own future in our hands. Let us reject therefore the policies of those who whine and whimper about our frustrations and call on us to turn inward.

Let us not turn away from greatness.

The chance America now has to lead the way to a lasting peace in the world may never come again.

With faith in God and faith in ourselves and faith in our country, let us have the vision and the courage to seize the moment and meet the challenge before it slips away.

On your television screen last night, you saw the cemetery in Leningrad I visited on my trip to the Soviet Union—where 300,000 people died in the siege of that city during World War II.

At the cemetery I saw the picture of a 12-year-old girl. She was a beautiful child. Her name was Tanya.

I read her diary. It tells the terrible story of war. In the simple words of a child she wrote of the deaths of the members of her family. Zhenya in December. Grannie in January. Then Leka. Then Uncle Vasya. Then Uncle Lyosha. Then Mama in May. And finally—these were the last words in her diary: "All are dead. Only Tanya is left."

Let us think of Tanya and of the other Tanyas and their brothers and sisters everywhere in Russia, in China, in America, as we proudly meet our responsibilities for leadership in the world in a way worthy of a great people.

I ask you, my fellow Americans, to join our new majority not just in the cause of winning an election, but in achieving a hope that mankind has had since the beginning of civilization. Let us build a peace that our children and all the children of the world can enjoy for generations to come.

27.

"There can be no whitewash at the White House" (April 30, 1973)

Nixon spoke on the unfolding Watergate scandal as infrequently as possible. That made this nationally televised address hardly three months after his triumphant second inauguration especially dramatic. It was an attempt to contain the scandal by firing his two closest White House aides, Bob Haldeman and John Ehrlichman, and appointing a new attorney general with the charge of "uncovering the whole truth" about Watergate. Politically, the scapegoating move helped; House minority leader Gerald Ford announced afterward, "I am absolutely positive he had nothing to do with this mess." But some Democratic politicians, noting that the president's extraordinary closeness to these two aides rendered this notion unlikely, began calling for impeachment proceedings. As well, a lesser-noticed portion of the speech—the firing of staff council John Dean, whom Nixon had publicly given the role of investigating the scandal, with the private role of helping cover it up—portended a dire outcome for Nixon: Dean's sworn testimony three months later relating, in great detail, Nixon's active involvement with "this mess." The speech below was full of outright fabrications—such as Nixon's claim that he had delegated reelection operations as much as possible. In fact, he micromanaged his campaign from the Oval Office more than any president before him.

Good evening:

I want to talk to you tonight from my heart on a subject of deep concern to every American.

In recent months, members of my Administration and officials of the Committee for the Re-Election of the President—including some of my closest friends and most trusted aides—have been charged with involvement in what has come to be known as the Watergate affair. These include charges of illegal activity during and preceding the 1972 Presidential election and charges that responsible officials participated in efforts to cover up that illegal activity.

The inevitable result of these charges has been to raise serious questions about the integrity of the White House itself. Tonight I wish to address those questions.

Last June 17, while I was in Florida trying to get a few days rest after my visit to Moscow, I first learned from news reports of the Watergate break-in. I was appalled at this senseless, illegal action, and I was shocked to learn that employees of the Re-Election Committee were apparently among those guilty. I immediately ordered an investigation by appropriate Government authorities. On

September 15, as you will recall, indictments were brought against seven defendants in the case.

As the investigations went forward, I repeatedly asked those conducting the investigation whether there was any reason to believe that members of my Administration were in any way involved. I received repeated assurances that there were not. Because of these continuing reassurances, because I believed the reports I was getting, because I had faith in the persons from whom I was getting them, I discounted the stories in the press that appeared to implicate members of my Administration or other officials of the campaign committee.

Until March of this year, I remained convinced that the denials were true and that the charges of involvement by members of the White House Staff were false. The comments I made during this period, and the comments made by my Press Secretary in my behalf, were based on the information provided to us at the time we made those comments. However, new information then came to me which persuaded me that there was a real possibility that some of these charges were true, and suggesting further that there had been an effort to conceal the facts both from the public, from you, and from me.

As a result, on March 21, I personally assumed the responsibility for coordinating intensive new inquiries into the matter, and I personally ordered those conducting the investigations to get all the facts and to report them directly to me, right here in this office.

I again ordered that all persons in the Government or at the Re-Election Committee should cooperate fully with the FBI, the prosecutors, and the grand jury. I also ordered that anyone who refused to cooperate in telling the truth would be asked to resign from Government service. And, with ground rules adopted that would preserve the basic constitutional separation of powers between the Congress and the Presidency, I directed that members of the White House Staff should appear and testify voluntarily under oath before the Senate committee which was investigating Watergate.

I was determined that we should get to the bottom of the matter, and that the truth should be fully brought out—no matter who was involved.

At the same time, I was determined not to take precipitate action and to avoid, if at all possible, any action that would appear to reflect on innocent people. I wanted to be fair. But I knew that in the final analysis, the integrity of this office—public faith in the integrity of this office—would have to take priority over all personal considerations.

Today, in one of the most difficult decisions of my Presidency, I accepted the resignations of two of my closest associates in the White House—Bob

Haldeman, John Ehrlichman—two of the finest public servants it has been my privilege to know.

I want to stress that in accepting these resignations, I mean to leave no implication whatever of personal wrongdoing on their part, and I leave no implication tonight of implication on the part of others who have been charged in this matter. But in matters as sensitive as guarding the integrity of our democratic process, it is essential not only that rigorous legal and ethical standards be observed but also that the public, you, have total confidence that they are both being observed and enforced by those in authority and particularly by the President of the United States. They agreed with me that this move was necessary in order to restore that confidence.

Because Attorney General Kleindienst—though a distinguished public servant, my personal friend for 20 years, with no personal involvement whatever in this matter—has been a close personal and professional associate of some of those who are involved in this case, he and I both felt that it was also necessary to name a new Attorney General.

The Counsel to the President, John Dean, has also resigned.

As the new Attorney General, I have today named Elliot Richardson, a man of unimpeachable integrity and rigorously high principle. I have directed him to do everything necessary to ensure that the Department of Justice has the confidence and the trust of every law-abiding person in this country.

I have given him absolute authority to make all decisions bearing upon the prosecution of the Watergate case and related matters. I have instructed him that if he should consider it appropriate, he has the authority to name a special supervising prosecutor for matters arising out of the case.

Whatever may appear to have been the case before, whatever improper activities may yet be discovered in connection with this whole sordid affair, I want the American people, I want you to know beyond the shadow of a doubt that during my term as President, justice will be pursued fairly, fully, and impartially, no matter who is involved. This office is a sacred trust and I am determined to be worthy of that trust.

Looking back at the history of this case, two questions arise:

How could it have happened?

Who is to blame?

Political commentators have correctly observed that during my 27 years in politics I have always previously insisted on running my own campaigns for office.

But 1972 presented a very different situation. In both domestic and foreign policy, 1972 was a year of crucially important decisions, of intense negotiations, of vital new directions, particularly in working toward the goal which has been my overriding concern throughout my political career—the goal of bringing peace to America, peace to the world.

That is why I decided, as the 1972 campaign approached, that the Presidency should come first and politics second. To the maximum extent possible, therefore, I sought to delegate campaign operations, to remove the day-to-day campaign decisions from the President's office and from the White House. I also, as you recall, severely limited the number of my own campaign appearances.

Who, then, is to blame for what happened in this case?

For specific criminal actions by specific individuals, those who committed those actions must, of course, bear the liability and pay the penalty.

For the fact that alleged improper actions took place within the White House or within my campaign organization, the easiest course would be for me to blame those to whom I delegated the responsibility to run the campaign. But that would be a cowardly thing to do.

I will not place the blame on subordinates—on people whose zeal exceeded their judgment and who may have done wrong in a cause they deeply believed to be right.

In any organization, the man at the top must bear the responsibility. That responsibility, therefore, belongs here, in this office. I accept it. And I pledge to you tonight, from this office, that I will do everything in my power to ensure that the guilty are brought to justice and that such abuses are purged from our political processes in the years to come, long after I have left this office.

Some people, quite properly appalled at the abuses that occurred, will say that Watergate demonstrates the bankruptcy of the American political system. I believe precisely the opposite is true. Watergate represented a series of illegal acts and bad judgments by a number of individuals. It was the system that has brought the facts to light and that will bring those guilty to justice—a system that in this case has included a determined grand jury, honest prosecutors, a courageous judge, John Sirica, and a vigorous free press.

It is essential now that we place our faith in that system—and especially in the judicial system. It is essential that we let the judicial process go forward, respecting those safeguards that are established to protect the innocent as well as to convict the guilty. It is essential that in reacting to the excesses of others, we not fall into excesses ourselves.

It is also essential that we not be so distracted by events such as this that we neglect the vital work before us, before this Nation, before America, at a time of critical importance to America and the world.

Since March, when I first learned that the Watergate affair might in fact be far more serious than I had been led to believe, it has claimed far too much of my time and my attention.

Whatever may now transpire in the case, whatever the actions of the grand jury, whatever the outcome of any eventual trials, I must now turn my full attention—and I shall do so—once again to the larger duties of this office. I owe it to this great office that I hold, and I owe it to you—to my country.

I know that as Attorney General, Elliot Richardson will be both fair and he will be fearless in pursuing this case wherever it leads. I am confident that with him in charge, justice will be done.

There is vital work to be done toward our goal of a lasting structure of peace in the world—work that cannot wait, work that I must do.

Tomorrow, for example, Chancellor Brandt of West Germany will visit the White House for talks that are a vital element of "The Year of Europe," as 1973 has been called. We are already preparing for the next Soviet-American summit meeting later this year.

This is also a year in which we are seeking to negotiate a mutual and balanced reduction of armed forces in Europe, which will reduce our defense budget and allow us to have funds for other purposes at home so desperately needed. It is the year when the United States and Soviet negotiators will seek to work out the second and even more important round of our talks on limiting nuclear arms and of reducing the danger of a nuclear war that would destroy civilization as we know it. It is a year in which we confront the difficult tasks of maintaining peace in Southeast Asia and in the potentially explosive Middle East.

There is also vital work to be done right here in America: to ensure prosperity, and that means a good job for everyone who wants to work; to control inflation, that I know worries every housewife, everyone who tries to balance a family budget in America; to set in motion new and better ways of ensuring progress toward a better life for all Americans.

When I think of this office—of what it means—I think of all the things that I want to accomplish for this Nation, of all the things I want to accomplish for you.

On Christmas Eve, during my terrible personal ordeal of the renewed bombing of North Vietnam, which after 12 years of war finally helped to bring America peace with honor, I sat down just before midnight. I wrote out some of my goals for my second term as President. Let me read them to you.

"To make it possible for our children, and for our children's children, to live in a world of peace.

"To make this country be more than ever a land of opportunity—of equal opportunity, full opportunity for every American.

"To provide jobs for all who can work, and generous help for those who cannot work.

"To establish a climate of decency and civility, in which each person respects the feelings and the dignity and the Godgiven rights of his neighbor.

"To make this a land in which each person can dare to dream, can live his dreams—not in fear, but in hope—proud of his community, proud of his country, proud of what America has meant to himself and to the world."

These are great goals. I believe we can, we must work for them. We can achieve them. But we cannot achieve these goals unless we dedicate ourselves to another goal.

We must maintain the integrity of the White House, and that integrity must be real, not transparent. There can be no whitewash at the White House.

We must reform our political process—ridding it not only of the violations of the law but also of the ugly mob violence and other inexcusable campaign tactics that have been too often practiced and too readily accepted in the past, including those that may have been a response by one side to the excesses or expected excesses of the other side. Two wrongs do not make a right.

I have been in public life for more than a quarter of a century. Like any other calling, politics has good people and bad people. And let me tell you, the great majority in politics—in the Congress, in the Federal Government, in the State government—are good people. I know that it can be very easy, under the intensive pressures of a campaign, for even well-intentioned people to fall into shady tactics—to rationalize this on the grounds that what is at stake is of such importance to the Nation that the end justifies the means. And both of our great parties have been guilty of such tactics in the past.

In recent years, however, the campaign excesses that have occurred on all sides have provided a sobering demonstration of how far this false doctrine can take us. The lesson is clear: America, in its political campaigns, must not again fall into the trap of letting the end, however great that end is, justify the means.

I urge the leaders of both political parties, I urge citizens, all of you, everywhere, to join in working toward a new set of standards, new rules and procedures to ensure that future elections will be as nearly free of such abuses as they possibly can be made. This is my goal. I ask you to join in making it America's goal.

When I was inaugurated for a second time this past January 20, I gave each member of my Cabinet and each member of my senior White House Staff a special 4-year calendar, with each day marked to show the number of days remaining to the Administration. In the inscription on each calendar, I wrote these words: "The Presidential term which begins today consists of 1,461 days—no more, no less. Each can be a day of strengthening and renewal for America; each can add depth and dimension to the American experience. If we strive together, if we make the most of the challenge and the opportunity that these days offer us, they can stand out as great days for America, and great moments in the history of the world."

I looked at my own calendar this morning up at Camp David as I was working on this speech. It showed exactly 1,361 days remaining in my term. I want these to be the best days in America's history, because I love America. I deeply believe that America is the hope of the world. And I know that in the quality and wisdom of the leadership America gives lies the only hope for millions of people all over the world that they can live their lives in peace and freedom. We must be worthy of that hope, in every sense of the word. Tonight, I ask for your prayers to help me in everything that I do throughout the days of my Presidency to be worthy of their hopes and of yours.

God bless America and God bless each and every one of you.

28.

"I am not a crook" (November 17, 1973)

In November of 1973, with his approval rating below 30 percent after his firing of special prosecutor Archibald Cox and the discovery that two White House tapes were missing, and with impeachment talk in the air, Nixon gave an hour-long televised question-and-answer session with four hundred Associated Press managing editors. Tensely, he lied that he had had no knowledge until the spring of 1973 of proposals to blackmail the burglars and that he was not involved in any cover-up, and he blamed the scandal on his not having supervised his campaign more closely. He also repeated a technique from the Checkers speech of 1952, right down to the detailed account of his assets and liabilities: faced with specific allegations about his finances in the context of his abuse of executive power, he reframed the charges as accusations about his personal financial probity generally. When he said, "I am not a crook," it was a reference to his self-exculpatory claim that he had not enriched himself in office.

Let me just respond, if I could, sir, before going to your question—I will turn left and then come back to the right; I don't want to tilt either way at the moment, as you can be sure—since the question was raised a moment ago about my tax payments.

I noted in some editorials and perhaps in some commentaries on television a very reasonable question. They said, you know, "How is it that President Nixon could have a very heavy investment in a fine piece of property in San Clemente and a big investment in a piece of property in Florida," in which I have two houses, one which I primarily use as an office and the other as a residence, and also an investment in what was my mother's home, not very much of a place but I do own it—those three pieces of property.

I want to say first, that is all I have. I am the first President since Harry Truman who hasn't owned any stock since ever I have been President. I am the first one who has not had a blind trust since Harry Truman. Now, that doesn't prove that those who owned stocks or had blind trusts did anything wrong. But I felt that in the Presidency it was important to have no question about the President's personal finances, and I thought real estate was the best place to put it.

But then, the question was raised by good editorial writers—and I want to respond to it because some of you might be too polite to ask such an embarrassing question—they said, "Now, Mr. President, you earned $800,000 when you were President. Obviously, you paid at least half that much or could have paid half that much in taxes or a great deal of it—how could you possibly have had the money? Where did you get it?"

And then, of course, overriding all of that is the story to the effect that I have a million dollars in campaign funds, which was broadly printed throughout this country with retractions not quite getting quite as much play as the printing of the first, and particularly not on television. The newspapers did much better than television in that respect, I should point out.

And second, they said, "How is it that as far as this money is concerned, how is it possible for you to have this kind of investment when all you earned was $800,000 as President?"

Well, I should point out I wasn't a pauper when I became President. I wasn't very rich as Presidents go. But you see, in the 8 years that I was out of office—first, just to put it all out and I will give you a paper on this, we will send it around to you, and these figures I would like you to have, not today, but I will have it in a few days—when I left office after 4 years as a Congressman, 2 years as a Senator, and 8 years at $45,000 a year as Vice President, and after stories had been written, particularly in the *Washington Post* to the effect that the [Vice] President had purchased a mansion in Wesley Heights and people wondered where the money came from, you know what my net worth was? Forty-seven thousand dollars total, after 14 years of Government service, and a 1958 Oldsmobile that needed an overhaul.

Now, I have no complaints. In the next 8 years, I made a lot of money. I made $250,000 from a book and the serial rights which many of you were good enough to purchase, also. In the practice of law—and I am not claiming I was worth it, but apparently former Vice Presidents or Presidents are worth a great deal to law firms—and I did work pretty hard.

But also in that period, I earned between $100,000 and $250,000 every year.

So that when I, in 1968, decided to become a candidate for President, I decided to clean the decks and to put everything in real estate. I sold all my stock for $300,000—that is all I owned. I sold my apartment in New York for $300,000—I am using rough figures here. And I had $100,000 coming to me from the law firm.

And so, that is where the money came from. Let me just say this, and I want to say this to the television audience: I made my mistakes, but in all of my years of public life, I have never profited, never profited from public service—I have earned every cent. And in all of my years of public life, I have never obstructed justice. And I think, too, that I could say that in my years of public life, that I welcome this kind of examination, because people have got to know whether or not their President is a crook. Well, I am not a crook. I have earned everything I have got.

29.

"I made clear there was to be no coverup" (April 29, 1974)

On July 16, 1973, a White House aide revealed in congressional testimony that Nixon tape-recorded every word uttered in his various offices. Nixon then announced his refusal to turn the tapes over to Watergate special prosecutor Archibald Cox. His explanation was "executive privilege"—that no other governmental agency had a right to hear advice given the president in confidence. In the spring of 1974 the House Judiciary Committee subpoenaed the tapes. Nixon claimed to be honoring the subpoena by turning over his own transcripts of the requested conversations, running to twelve hundred pages. In doing so, he declared his innocence, claiming the tapes exonerated him.

In this address, he gave his own, highly distorted version of their contents, dwelling especially on those moments he claimed showed he had no knowledge of any cover-up until the spring of 1973—which was, in reality, nine months after he began directing the cover-up from the Oval Office. He twisted the charge against him to reduce it to the single allegation—that he had promised clemency to the defendants—and pointed to moments where he had specifically refused to offer clemency. These claims, however, did not survive the exposure of the fuller record, and the quotations he pointed to were shown in retrospect to be a yet more fiendish turn in the cover-up: an attempt to place faked exculpatory evidence on the taped record, in the hopes he could contain public exposure of the tapes to those specific moments.

John Dean charged in sworn Senate testimony that I was "fully aware of the coverup" at the time of our first meeting on September 15, 1972. These transcripts show clearly that I first learned of it when Mr. Dean himself told me about it in this office on March 21—some 6 months later.

Incidentally, these transcripts—covering hours upon hours of conversations—should place in somewhat better perspective the controversy over the 18½ minute gap in the tape of a conversation I had with Mr. Haldeman back in June of 1972.

Now, how it was caused is still a mystery to me and, I think, to many of the experts as well. But I am absolutely certain, however, of one thing: that it was not caused intentionally by my secretary, Rose Mary Woods, or any of my White House assistants. And certainly, if the theory were true that during those 18½ minutes, Mr. Haldeman and I cooked up some sort of a Watergate coverup scheme, as so many have been quick to surmise, it hardly seems likely that in all of our subsequent conversations—many of them are here—which neither of us ever expected would see the light of day, there is nothing remotely indicating such a scheme; indeed, quite the contrary.

From the beginning, I have said that in many places on the tapes there were ambiguities—a statement and comments that different people with different perspectives might interpret in drastically different ways—but although the words may be ambiguous, though the discussions may have explored many alternatives, the record of my actions is totally clear now, and I still believe it was totally correct then.

A prime example is one of the most controversial discussions, that with Mr. Dean on March 21—the one in which he first told me of the coverup, with Mr. Haldeman joining us midway through the conversation.

His revelations to me on March 21 were a sharp surprise, even though the report he gave to me was far from complete, especially since he did not reveal at that time the extent of his own criminal involvement.

I was particularly concerned by his report that one of the Watergate defendants, Howard Hunt, was threatening blackmail unless he and his lawyer were immediately given $121,000 for legal fees and family support, and that he was attempting to blackmail the White House, not by threatening exposure on the Watergate matter, but by threatening to reveal activities that would expose extremely sensitive, highly secret national security matters that he had worked on before Watergate.

I probed, questioned, tried to learn all Mr. Dean knew about who was involved, what was involved. I asked more than 150 questions of Mr. Dean in the course of that conversation.

He said to me, and I quote from the transcripts directly: "I can just tell from our conversation that these are things that you have no knowledge of."

It was only considerably later that I learned how much there was that he did not tell me then—for example, that he himself had authorized promises of clemency, that he had personally handled money for the Watergate defendants, and that he had suborned perjury of a witness.

I knew that I needed more facts. I knew that I needed the judgments of more people. I knew the facts about the Watergate coverup would have to be made public, but I had to find out more about what they were before I could decide how they could best be made public.

I returned several times to the immediate problem posed by Mr. Hunt's blackmail threat, which to me was not a Watergate problem, but one which I regarded, rightly or wrongly, as a potential national security problem of very serious proportions. I considered long and hard whether it might in fact be better to let the payment go forward, at least temporarily, in the hope that this national security matter would not be exposed in the course of uncovering the Watergate coverup.

I believed then, and I believe today, that I had a responsibility as President to consider every option, including this one, where production of sensitive national security matters was at issue—protection of such matters. In the course of considering it and of "just thinking out loud," as I put it at one point, I several times suggested that meeting Hunt's demands might be necessary.

But then I also traced through where that would lead. The money could be raised. But money demands would lead inescapably to clemency demands, and clemency could not be granted. I said, and I quote directly from the tape: "It is wrong, that's for sure." I pointed out, and I quote again from the tape: "But in the end we are going to be bled to death. And in the end it is all going to come out anyway. Then you get the worst of both worlds. We are going to lose, and people are going to—"

And Mr. Haldeman interrupts me and says: "And look like dopes!"

And I responded, "And in effect look like a coverup. So that we cannot do."

Now, I recognize that this tape of March 21 is one which different meanings could be read in by different people. But by the end of the meeting, as the tape shows, my decision was to convene a new grand jury and to send everyone before the grand jury with instructions to testify.

Whatever the potential for misinterpretation there may be as a result of the different options that were discussed at different times during the meeting, my conclusion at the end of the meeting was clear. And my actions and reactions as demonstrated on the tapes that follow that date show clearly that I did not intend the further payment to Hunt or anyone else be made. These are some of the actions that I took in the weeks that followed in my effort to find the truth, to carry out my responsibilities to enforce the law:

As a tape of our meeting on March 22, the next day, indicates, I directed Mr. Dean to go to Camp David with instructions to put together a written report. I learned 5 days later, on March 26, that he was unable to complete it. And so on March 27, I assigned John Ehrlichman to try to find out what had happened, who was at fault, and in what ways and to what degree.

One of the transcripts I am making public is a call that Mr. Ehrlichman made to the Attorney General on March 28, in which he asked the Attorney General to report to me, the President, directly, any information he might find indicating possible involvement of John Mitchell or by anyone in the White House. I had Mr. Haldeman separately pursue other, independent lines of inquiry.

Throughout, I was trying to reach determinations on matters of both substance and procedure on what the facts were and what was the best way to move the case forward. I concluded that I wanted everyone to go before the grand jury and testify freely and fully. This decision, as you will recall, was publicly announced on March 30, 1973. I waived executive privilege in order to permit everybody to testify. I specifically waived executive privilege with regard to conversations with the President, and I waived the attorney-client privilege with John Dean in order to permit him to testify fully and, I hope, truthfully.

Finally, on April 14—3 weeks after I learned of the coverup from Mr. Dean—Mr. Ehrlichman reported to me on the results of his investigation. As he acknowledged, much of what he had gathered was hearsay, but he had gathered enough to make it clear that the next step was to make his findings completely available to the Attorney General, which I instructed him to do.

And the next day, Sunday, April 15, Attorney General Kleindienst asked to see me, and he reported new information which had come to his attention on this matter. And although he was in no way whatever involved in Watergate, because of his close personal ties, not only to John Mitchell but to other potential people who might be involved, he quite properly removed himself from the case.

We agreed that Assistant Attorney General Henry Petersen, the head of the Criminal Division, a Democrat and career prosecutor, should be placed in complete charge of the investigation.

Later that day, I met with Mr. Petersen. I continued to meet with him, to talk with him, to consult with him, to offer him the full cooperation of the White House—as you will see from these transcripts—even to the point of retaining John Dean on the White House Staff for an extra week after he admitted his criminal involvement, because Mr. Petersen thought that would make it easier for the prosecutor to get his cooperation in breaking the case if it should become necessary to grant Mr. Dean's demand for immunity.

On April 15, when I heard that one of the obstacles to breaking the case was Gordon Liddy's refusal to talk, I telephoned Mr. Petersen and directed that he should make clear not only to Mr. Liddy but to everyone that—and now I quote directly from the tape of that telephone call—"As far as the President is concerned, everybody in this case is to talk and to tell the truth." I told him if necessary I would personally meet with Mr. Liddy's lawyer to assure him that I wanted Liddy to talk and to tell the truth.

From the time Mr. Petersen took charge, the case was solidly within the criminal justice system, pursued personally by the Nation's top professional prosecutor with the active, personal assistance of the President of the United States.

I made clear there was to be no coverup.

Let me quote just a few lines from the transcripts—you can read them to verify them—so that you can hear for yourself the orders I was giving in this period.

Speaking to Haldeman and Ehrlichman, I said: ". . . It is ridiculous to talk about clemency. They all knew that."

Speaking to Ehrlichman, I said: "We all have to do the right thing . . . We just cannot have this kind of a business . . ."

Speaking to Haldeman and Ehrlichman, I said: "The boil had to be pricked . . . We have to prick the boil and take the heat. Now that's what we are doing here."

Speaking to Henry Petersen, I said: "I want you to be sure to understand that you know we are going to get to the bottom of this thing."

Speaking to John Dean, I said: "Tell the truth. That is the thing I have told everybody around here."

And then speaking to Haldeman: "And you tell Magruder, 'now Jeb, this evidence is coming in, you ought to go to the grand jury. Purge yourself if you're perjured and tell this whole story.'"

I am confident that the American people will see these transcripts for what they are, fragmentary records from a time more than a year ago that now seems very distant, the records of a President and of a man suddenly being confronted and having to cope with information which, if true, would have the most far-reaching consequences, not only for his personal reputation but, more important, for his hopes, his plans, his goals for the people who had elected him as their leader.

If read with an open and a fair mind and read together with the record of the actions I took, these transcripts will show that what I have stated from the beginning to be the truth has been the truth: that I personally had no knowledge of the break-in before it occurred, that I had no knowledge of the coverup until I was informed of it by John Dean on March 21, that I never offered clemency for the defendants, and that after March 21, my actions were directed toward finding the facts and seeing that justice was done, fairly and according to the law.

The facts are there. The conversations are there. The record of actions is there.

To anyone who reads his way through this mass of materials I have provided, it will be totally, abundantly clear that as far as the President's role with regard to Watergate is concerned, the entire story is there. . . .

30.

"My mother was a saint" (August 9, 1974)

The end came quickly. The Supreme Court unanimously ruled that Nixon had to turn over tape recordings of sixty-four White House conversations. Three days later, the House Judiciary Committee passed the first article of impeachment, on obstruction of justice. A group of Republican legislators led by Barry Goldwater informed him he didn't have the votes in the Senate to beat the charges. Nixon became the first president to resign. Before the flight that bore him to California and ignominy, he gave the following rambling statement to White House staff—his last speech as president.

Members of the Cabinet, members of the White House Staff, all of our friends here:

I think the record should show that this is one of those spontaneous things that we always arrange whenever the President comes in to speak, and it will be so reported in the press, and we don't mind, because they have to call it as they see it.

But on our part, believe me, it is spontaneous.

You are here to say goodby to us, and we don't have a good word for it in English—the best is au revoir. We will see you again.

I just met with the members of the White House staff, you know, those who serve here in the White House day in and day out, and I asked them to do what I ask all of you to do to the extent that you can and, of course, are requested to do so: to serve our next President as you have served me and previous Presidents—because many of you have been here for many years—with devotion and dedication, because this office, great as it is, can only be as great as the men and women who work for and with the President.

This house, for example—I was thinking of it as we walked down this hall, and I was comparing it to some of the great houses of the world that I have been in. This isn't the biggest house. Many, and most, in even smaller countries, are much bigger. This isn't the finest house. Many in Europe, particularly, and in China, Asia, have paintings of great, great value, things that we just don't have here and, probably, will never have until we are 1,000 years old or older.

But this is the best house. It is the best house, because it has something far more important than numbers of people who serve, far more important than numbers of rooms or how big it is, far more important than numbers of magnificent pieces of art.

This house has a great heart, and that heart comes from those who serve. I was rather sorry they didn't come down. We said goodby to them upstairs. But they are really great. And I recall after so many times I have made speeches, and some of them pretty tough, yet, I always come back, or after a hard day—and my days usually have run rather long—I would always get a lift from them, because I might be a little down but they always smiled.

And so it is with you. I look around here, and I see so many on this staff that, you know, I should have been by your offices and shaken hands, and I would love to have talked to you and found out how to run the world—everybody wants to tell the President what to do, and boy, he needs to be told many times—but I just haven't had the time. But I want you to know that each and every one of you, I know, is indispensable to this Government.

I am proud of this Cabinet. I am proud of all the members who have served in our Cabinet. I am proud of our sub-Cabinet. I am proud of our White House Staff. As I pointed out last night, sure, we have done some things wrong in this Administration, and the top man always takes the responsibility, and I have never ducked it. But I want to say one thing: We can be proud of it—5 ½ years. No man or no woman came into this Administration and left it with more of this world's goods than when he came in. No man or no woman ever profited at the public expense or the public till. That tells something about you.

Mistakes, yes. But for personal gain, never. You did what you believed in. Sometimes right, sometimes wrong. And I only wish that I were a wealthy man—at the present time, I have got to find a way to pay my taxes—[laughter]—and if I were, I would like to recompense you for the sacrifices that all of you have made to serve in government.

But you are getting something in government—and I want you to tell this to your children, and I hope the Nation's children will hear it, too—something in government service that is far more important than money. It is a cause bigger than yourself. It is the cause of making this the greatest nation in the world, the leader of the world, because without our leadership, the world will know nothing but war, possibly starvation or worse, in the years ahead. With our leadership it will know peace, it will know plenty.

We have been generous, and we will be more generous in the future as we are able to. But most important, we must be strong here, strong in our hearts, strong in our souls, strong in our belief, and strong in our willingness to sacrifice, as you have been willing to sacrifice, in a pecuniary way, to serve in government.

There is something else I would like for you to tell your young people. You know, people often come in and say, "What will I tell my kids?" They look at government and say, sort of a rugged life, and they see the mistakes that are made. They get the impression that everybody is here for the purpose of feathering his nest. That is why I made this earlier point—not in this Administration, not one single man or woman.

And I say to them, there are many fine careers. This country needs good farmers, good businessmen, good plumbers, good carpenters.

I remember my old man. I think that they would have called him sort of a little man, common man. He didn't consider himself that way. You know what he was? He was a streetcar motorman first, and then he was a farmer, and then he had a lemon ranch. It was the poorest lemon ranch in California, I can assure you. He sold it before they found oil on it. [Laughter] And then he was a grocer. But he was a great man, because he did his job, and every job counts up to the hilt, regardless of what happens.

Nobody will ever write a book, probably, about my mother. Well, I guess all of you would say this about your mother—my mother was a saint. And I think of her, two boys dying of tuberculosis, nursing four others in order that she could take care of my older brother for 3 years in Arizona, and seeing each of them die, and when they died, it was like one of her own.

Yes, she will have no books written about her. But she was a saint.

Now, however, we look to the future. I had a little quote in the speech last night from T.R. As you know, I kind of like to read books. I am not educated, but I do read books—[laughter]—and the T.R. quote was a pretty good one. Here is another one I found as I was reading, my last night in the White House, and this quote is about a young man. He was a young lawyer in New York. He had married a beautiful girl, and they had a lovely daughter, and then suddenly she died, and this is what he wrote. This was in his diary.

He said, "She was beautiful in face and form and lovelier still in spirit. As a flower she grew and as a fair young flower she died. Her life had been always in the sunshine. There had never come to her a single great sorrow. None ever knew her who did not love and revere her for her bright and sunny temper and her saintly unselfishness. Fair, pure and joyous as a maiden, loving, tender and happy as a young wife. When she had just become a mother, when her life seemed to be just begun and when the years seemed so bright before her, then by a strange and terrible fate death came to her. And when my heart's dearest died, the light went from my life forever."

That was T.R. in his twenties. He thought the light had gone from his life forever—but he went on. And he not only became President but, as an ex-President, he served his country, always in the arena, tempestuous, strong, sometimes wrong, sometimes right, but he was a man.

And as I leave, let me say, that is an example I think all of us should remember. We think sometimes when things happen that don't go the right way; we think that when you don't pass the bar exam the first time—I happened to, but I was just lucky; I mean, my writing was so poor the bar examiner said, "We have just got to let the guy through." We think that when someone dear to us dies, we think that when we lose an election, we think that when we suffer a defeat that all is ended. We think, as T.R. said, that the light had left his life forever.

Not true. It is only a beginning, always. The young must know it; the old must know it. It must always sustain us, because the greatness comes not when things go always good for you, but the greatness comes and you are really tested, when you take some knocks, some disappointments, when sadness comes, because only if you have been in the deepest valley can you ever know how magnificent it is to be on the highest mountain.

And so I say to you on this occasion, as we leave, we leave proud of the people who have stood by us and worked for us and served this country.

We want you to be proud of what you have done. We want you to continue to serve in government, if that is your wish. Always give your best, never get discouraged, never be petty; always remember, others may hate you, but those who hate you don't win unless you hate them, and then you destroy yourself.

And so, we leave with high hopes, in good spirit, and with deep humility, and with very much gratefulness in our hearts. I can only say to each and every one of you, we come from many faiths, we pray perhaps to different gods—but really the same God in a sense—but I want to say for each and every one of you, not only will we always remember you, not only will we always be grateful to you but always you will be in our hearts and you will be in our prayers.

Thank you very much.

Index

Aberdeen Arsenal, 36
Abrams, Creighton, 182, 204
Abt, John, 23, 30
Acheson, Dean, xxvii, xxx, 41, 52
Adams, Sherman, 71
Agnew, Spiro, lx, 209
Aid to Families with Dependent Children, 163, 166
Aiken, George, lv
Ailes, Roger, xliv
Air Force Academy commencement speech (Nixon), 153
Alsop, Joseph, xxiv
Amerasia case, 62
American Civil Liberties Union (ACLU), lviii
American Communist Party, xxiv
American Dream, 149, 157
American Indians, 115
American politics, practical nature of, ix
antiwar sentiment, lviii; Nixon on, 170, 187–88, 206–8, 210; protests, 200–201; scientists, lix; senators, lix
"Appraisal from Manila" (Nixon), 117–20
Asia, 128–44, 180–82. See also *individual countries*
"Asia after Viet Nam" (Nixon), xiii, xv, lii, 128–44
Australia, 131

balance of power, li, lii
Bangladesh, liii
Barker, Bernard, 233, 235
Barnum, Everett, 4
Bay of Pigs, Cuba, 233, 235, 237
Bentley, Elizabeth, 20–21, 38
Berle, A. A., 26, 41–43, 53
Bernstein, Carl, 233
Beyond Peace (Nixon), lxvi
Brandt, Willy, 250
Bretton Woods Conference, 44
Brookings Institution, lx
Brown, Edmund "Pat," 106–7, 110–11
Bunker, Ellsworth, 204
Burma, 132, 139
Burns, Arthur, xlix
Bush, George W., lxvii
busing, 113

California governorship, Nixon's campaign for, xxxv–xxxvi
Cambodia, lvii, 200, 202, 204–6, 227

campaign tactics: moderation of, xxx, xxxiii–xxxv, 97–101; Nixon on, 253; Nixon's control of, 242–43, 247–48; opportunism in, xxxviii–xli; shrewdness of, xliii–xliv, 238; underhandedness of, xxiii–xxiv, xxxviii–xxxix, lix, lxi–lxii, 60–63, 117, 209–10; and Watergate, 242–43, 247–48
Campbell, Alexander, 32, 50
Canada, 213
capitalism, Communism compared to, 88–96
Caracas, Venezuela, xxxi
Carnegie Foundation for International Peace, 23, 49
Carswell, G. Harrold, 209–13
Castro, Fidel, 232–33
Central Americans, 115
Central Intelligence Agency (CIA), lix, 233, 237
Chambers, Whittaker, xxv–xxvi, 21–43, 50–53
"Checkers Speech" (Nixon), xxi–xxiii, 64–79, 255
China: Asian nations and, 129–30, 133–34, 143; balance of power and, lii; espionage concerning, 39–40; Kissinger and, lii, liii, 223, 224; Nixon and, xiii, xv, liii, lxvii, 108, 128, 141–44, 223–31; nuclear weapons of, 193; and "One China" communiqué, 223–31; and peace, 239, 241; Soviet Union's relationship with, li, lii, 192–93; and Taiwan, 223, 229–30; U.S. relations with, liii, 223–24, 228–31; and Vietnam, 173
Chi P'engfei, 224
Chotiner, Murray, xxiii
Chou En-lai, 224
Civil Aeronautics Board, xlvii
civil rights: backlash against, xl, xlii; 1968 election and, xl; 1964 election and, xxxvii–xxxviii; 1966 election and, xlii; Nixon and, xxxviii, xl, xlviii, 113–16, 124; school segregation and, xxxviii, 113–16
clemency, for Watergate participants, 259, 262, 263, 267
Clinton, Bill, lxvii
code, American secret, 36
Cold War, xxix, xxxi–xxxii, li, 88–96
Collins, Henry, 23, 30
Colson, Chuck, lxi, 233–34
Committee for the Re-Election of the President, 243, 245
common people: liberals and, xxii; Nixon and,

xxi–xxiii, xxvi, 77; Republicans and, xxii; stereotype of, lxviii. *See also* Silent Majority
Communism: in Asia, xxx; capitalism compared to, 88–96; decline of, li; espionage by Americans on behalf of, 21–23, 32, 35–59, 83–84; Hiss case and, xxv–xxvii, 19–59; international, 192–93; loyalty checks and, 57, 61, 83–87; Nixon and, xiii–xiv, xxiv, xxvii, xxx, xxxii, 7, 19, 56–63, 83–96; threat from, 42; Truman administration response to, 53–55; Vietnam and, 173–74, 176
Congress of Industrial Organizations, 36
Conley, Elmo H., 72
Connally, John, 219
Council of Foreign Relations, xiii
Cox, Archibald, 255, 259
crime. *See* law and order
Cuba, 108, 109, 232–37
Czechoslovakia, 193

Daily People's World (newspaper), 62
Dean, John, lxiv, lxvii, 242, 246, 260–62, 264–68
"Deep Throat," 233
Democratic National Committee, lvii, lxii, 232
Democratic Party: and economy, xlviii–l, 217; and law and order, xliv, 209; Nixon and, xxvii, lxi–lxii, 238–41, 242
Democrats for Nixon, 238
Dole, Bob, lxviii
domestic policy: civil rights, xlviii; drugs, xlv; economy, xlviii–l, 217–22; environment, xlvi; executive power and, xlvi–xlvii; Kennedy v. Nixon debate and, 98–101; law and order, xliii–xliv, 113–16, 121–27, 145–49, 209, 213–16; monetary policy, xlix, 218–20; Nixon's attitude toward, xliv–xlv; poverty, xlv, 163–69; race, xiv–xv, xxxviii, 113–16; Watergate and, 251
Domestic Policy Council, xlvii
domino theory, 129
Douglas, Helen Gahagan, xxiv, 60–63
Douglas, Melvyn, xxiv
drug control policies, xlv
Dulles, John Foster, 58
Dumbarton Oaks Conference (1944), 58

Eastern Europeans, 115
East Germany, 193
economy: Asian, 139–40; China-U.S. trade and,

economy *(cont.)* 230–31; U.S., xlviii–l, 217–22
Edson, Peter, 66–67
education, 57–58
Ehrlichman, John, xlvii, 242, 246, 264–65, 267
Eisenhower, Dwight D., xxi, xxviii–xxx, 64–65, 71, 99–100, 115, 173, 175
Electric Boat Co., 36
elites. *See* liberal elites
Ellsberg, Daniel, lx–lxi
Environmental Protection Agency, xlvi
Evans, Rowland, xl
executive privilege, 259, 265

family assistance program, xlv, 163–69
Federal Bureau of Investigation (FBI): and Hiss case, 43, 50, 55; Nixon's defense of, 55–56; and Watergate, 232–33, 236–37, 245
Federal Communications Commission (FCC), xlvii, 106
federal government, dismissals/resignations of workers for, 83–87
Federalist Papers, ix
Federal Maritime Administration, xlvii
Felt, Mark, 233, 236
Fillmore, Millard, lxvii
"The first civil right of every American is to be free from domestic violence" (Nixon), 145–49
food stamps, 163
Ford, Gerald, lxvii–lxviii, 242
Foreign Affairs (journal), xiii
foreign policy: Asia, 128–44; balance of power, li, lii; China, xiii, xv, liii, 128, 141–44, 223–31; control as goal of, li–lii; cruelty in, lii–liii; executive power and, l, lix; geopolitics and, 136–37, 191–99; Indonesia, lii–liii; Kennedy v. Nixon debate and, xxxiv, 97–98; "Kitchen Debate" and, 88–96; military intervention, 128, 134–36, 180–82; Nixon and, xxix–xxx, lii, lv, lxvi–lxviii; Nixon Doctrine, 128, 180–82; non-Western forms of government, 138; peace, lii, lvi, 95–96, 154–55, 159–62, 172–73, 175–80, 186, 188–90, 194–203, 205–6, 218, 225, 238–41, 248, 250, 251; postpresidency, lxvi–lxvii; Republican Party and, xxix; Soviet Union, liii, 88–96, 238, 250–51; stability in world order, li, lii, 136–37;

travel and, xiii, xxix–xxxii, liii, 88, 223–24; Vietnam War, xli, xliii, liv–lvi, 117–20, 170–90, 200–208; Watergate and, 250–51
"four b's," 14–15
FOX News, xliv
Frankfurter, Felix, 41, 52
Franklin Society, xx–xxi, 14
freedom, 198

Gandhi, Mahatma, lii, 195, 197, 198
Gannon, Frank, 14–16
Garment, Leonard, xli
Geneva Accords, 202
genocide, liii
"Gentlemen, this is my last press conference" (Nixon), xxxvi, 105–12
geopolitics, 191–99
Gesell, Harold, 39
Gibson, Dunn, & Crutcher, 71–72
God, 159, 161, 240, 276
gold, xlix, 219
Goldwater, Barry, x, xxxvii–xl, 113, 269
governorship of California, Nixon's campaign for, xxxv–xxxvi, 105–12
Gray, Pat, 233, 236
"The great silent majority of my fellow Americans" (Nixon), xxii, 170–90
Greek-Turkish Aid Bill, 61–62
Greenberg, Carl, 107–8
Groves, Leslie, 44–45
guaranteed income, 168–69
Guzenko, Igor, 46

Haldeman, Bob, xlviii, 232–37, 242, 245–46, 260–61, 263–64, 267
Han tribes, 132
Harriman, W. Averell, xxiv
Haynsworth, Clement, 209–13
"He can undisappear if we want him to" (Nixon), 232–37
"Her name was Tanya" (Nixon), 238–41
Hiss, Alger, xxiv–xxvii, 19–59, 78–79, 83, 106
Hiss, Donald, 23
"The Hiss Case—A Lesson for the American People" (Nixon), xxvi, 19–59
Hitler-Stalin pact, 36, 41–43, 53
Ho Chi Minh, 178–79
Hollywood Ten, xxi
Hong Kong, 139
Hoover, J. Edgar, 55
House Judiciary Committee, 259, 269
House un-American Activities Committee (HUAC), xxi, xxv, 19–59, 61
housing, 91–93
humiliation: national, 170, 175, 190, 202, 205–6;

humiliation *(cont.)*
Nixon's efforts at, xvi, xxx; personal, xvi, 105
Humphrey, Hubert, lxii
Hungary, 193
Hunt, Howard, 232–33, 235–36, 261–64
Huston, Tom Charles, lviii, lx

"I am not a crook" (Nixon), 255–58
Illinois Steel Company, 36
"I made clear there was to be no coverup" (Nixon), 259–68
impeachment, lxiv, 255, 269
Inaugural Address (1969), 153–62
India, 58, 130, 132, 138, 139, 195–98, 226, 228
Indochina, 225–26
Indonesia, lii, 130
Internal Revenue Service (IRS), lix
internationalism, xxix
Interstate Commerce Commission, xlvii
"The irresponsible tactics of some of the extreme civil rights leaders" (Nixon), 113–16
isolationism, xxix
"It's time for the great silent majority of this country to stand up and be counted" (Nixon), 213–16

Jammu, 226, 228
Japan, 139–40, 192, 226, 228
Jessup, Philip C., 53
Johnson, Lyndon, xxxix, xli–xlii, 117–18, 172–73, 175
judicial appointments, xlviii, 209–14
justice, rights concerning, 9

Kashmir, 226, 228
Kaufman, Samuel H., 52
Kennedy, John F., xxxiii–xxxiv, xxxvii, 97–101, 108, 153, 173–75
Kennedy, Robert F., xliii
Kennedy, Rose, lxv
Kent State University, 200–201, 207–8
Khan, Yahya, liii
Khrushchev, Nikita, xxxii–xxxiv, 88–96, 108
"kick around" speech, xxxvi, 105–12
King, Martin Luther, Jr., xliii
Kipling, Rudyard, 130
Kissinger, Henry: background of, l–li; character and personality of, li; and China, lii, liii, 223, 224; Nixon's relationship with, l–li, lvii–lviii; and secrecy,

l; and Vietnam War, lvi, 177; wiretap arranged by, lvii
"Kitchen Debate" (Nixon), xxxii, 88–96
kitchens, 91–92
Klein, Herb, 106
Kleindienst, Richard, 246, 265
Kleppe, Tom, 215
Kozlov, Frol, 90
Kraft, Joseph, lvii
Kuchel, Thomas, 111
Kulakov (Soviet lieutenant), 46
Ky, Ngo Cao, 117

Laird, Melvin, 182
Laos, 202, 204, 227
Latin America, liv
law and order, xliii–xliv, 113–16, 121–27, 145–49, 209, 213–16
Leaders (Nixon), lxvi
Letters, 5–6
Levine, Isaac Don, 41
Lewinsky, Monica, xxvi
liberal elites: and common people, xxii; Nixon and, xiv–xvii, xxiii–xxiv, xlv–xlvi, 65; stereotype of, lxviii
Liddy, Gordon, 266
Lima, Peru, xxxi
Lincoln, Abraham, xxi, 10, 77, 114, 115, 127, 240
Lippmann, Walter, xxiii
Lodge, Henry Cabot, Jr., xxxiv, 176, 177, 179
Los Angeles Times (newspaper), 107, 111
loyalty checks, 57, 61, 84

MacLeish, Archibald, 162
MacMillan, Margaret, liii
Magruder, Jeb, 267
Malaysia, 130, 140
Manila communiqué (1966), 117–20
Mao Zedong, 223, 224
Marcantonio, Vito, xxiv, 60–63
Marshall Plan, xxix
McCarthy, Joseph, xxxv, 19, 83
McCord, James, 232–33, 235–36
McCulloch, Bill, 114
McGovern, George, lxii
Medicaid, 163
Medina (judge), 55
Meet the Press (radio program), 31
Meet the Press (television program), 66
Mexicans, 115
Middle East, 251
military intervention, 128, 134–36, 180–82
Mitchell, John, 264–65
Mitchell, Stephen, 76
monetary policy, xlix, 218–20
Montagnards, 132

Morgenthau, Henry, 40
Moynihan, Daniel Patrick, xlv
Mundt, Karl, 24
Murphy, Thomas, 33
"My mother was a saint" (Nixon), 269–76

National Archives, lxvii
National Association for the Advancement of Colored People (NAACP), lviii
National Guard, 200–201
nationalism, 132
National Lawyers Guild, 55
national security, Watergate and, 261–63
National Security Council, xxxiii, l, lvii, 204
New Deal, xxii
New York Daily Worker (newspaper), 62
New York Times (newspaper), xlii, lvii, 191
New Zealand, 131
1956 election, xxviii–xxx
1960 election, xxxiii–xxxv
1968 election, xiii, xl–xliv, 145–49
1972 election, lxi–lxiii
1999: Victory without War (Nixon), lxvi
Nixon, Frank (father), xvii–xviii, lxv, 148, 273
Nixon, Hannah (mother), xix–xx, lii, lxv, 149, 273
Nixon, Harold (brother), xix
Nixon, Julie (daughter), 75, 149
Nixon, Pat (wife), 69, 73–76, 149, 224, 231
Nixon, Richard Milhous: assassination attempt against, xxxi; birth of, xvii, 3, 73; brothers of, xix; campaign fund accusations against, xxi, 64, 66; character and personality of, xvi–xvii, xx–xxi, xxv, xxxi, xliv, 3, 5; college years of, xx–xxi, 14–16, 73; in Congress, xxi–xxvii, 19–79; control as goal of, xvi–xvii, xliv, l, lvi, lxiv; and debate team, xviii–xix; and Democratic Party, xxvii, lxi–lxii, 238–41, 242; financial history of, 72–75, 255–58; funeral of, lxvii; and humiliation, xvi, xxx, 105, 170, 175, 190, 202, 205–6; ideological inconsistencies of, x, xiii–xvii, xxxvii–xli, 7, 113; illicit operations under, lvii–lxiv, 232–37, 242–54; Kissinger's relationship with, l–li, lvii–lviii; legacy of, lxviii–lxix; liberal aspects of, xlv–xlvi, lxvii; military service of, 73; music tastes of, 94; personality of (*see* character and personality of); politics of,

ix–x, xxii–xxiv, 64; presidency of, x–xi, xliv–lxvi, lxvii, 153–276; as presidential candidate, xxxi–xxxv; and Republican Party, x, xxvi, xxviii, xxxv, xxxvii–xli, 65, 114–16; reputation of, lxvii–lxviii; resentments of, x, xvi, xx–xxii, xxvi, xxxvi, lx–lxi, lxvi–lxvii, 78–79, 105, 110–12, 153; and sophisticates, xxi–xxii, xxiv, xxvi, lxv, 121 (*see also* liberal elites); storytelling abilities of, 3; "two Nixons," xv–xvii, 153 (*see also* ideological inconsistencies of); and vice presidency, xxi–xxiii, xxviii–xxxi, 65–79, 83–101; youth of, xvii–xx, xxix, 3–6, 73, 148–49. *See also* Nixon, Richard Milhous, writings and speeches of

Nixon, Richard Milhous, writings and speeches of: Air Force Academy commencement speech, 153; "Appraisal from Manila," 117–20; "Asia after Viet Nam," xiii, xv, lii, 128–44; *Beyond Peace*, lxvi; "Checkers Speech," xxi–xxiii, 64–79, 255; "The first civil right of every American is to be free from domestic violence," 145–49; Gannon interviews, 14–16; "Gentlemen, this is my last press conference," xxxvi, 105–12; "The great silent majority of my fellow Americans," xxii, 170–90; "He can undisappear if we want him to," 232–37; "Her name was Tanya," 238–41; "The Hiss Case–A Lesson for the American People," xxvi, 19–59; "I am not a crook," 255–58; "I made clear there was to be no coverup," 259–68; "The irresponsible tactics of some of the extreme civil rights leaders," 113–16; "It's time for the great silent majority of this country to stand up and be counted," 213–16; "kick around" speech, xxxvi, 105–12; "Kitchen Debate," xxxii, 88–96; *Leaders*, lxvi; memoirs, xi, xxxvii, 3–4, 105; "My mother was a saint," 269–76; *1999: Victory without War*, lxvi; *No More Vietnams*, lxvi; "One China," 223–31; Opening Statement, Kennedy v. Nixon Debate (1960), 97–101; "Our

Nixon, Richard *(cont.)*
best days lie ahead," 217–22; "Our Privileges under the Constitution," 7–13; "Pink Sheet," 60–63; "A pitiful, helpless giant," 203–6; "The postwar period in international relations has ended," 191–99; "The present welfare system has to be judged a colossal failure," 163–69; *The Real War*, lxvi; *RN: The Memoirs of Richard Nixon*, 3–4; *Seize the Moment*, lxvi; "Silent Majority" speech, xxii, 170–90; *Six Crises*, xxvi, xxxvii, liv, 105; "State of the World" message, 191–99; "There can be no whitewash at the White House," 242–54; "Those bums . . . blowing up the campuses," 206–7; "To lower our voices would be a simple thing," 153–62; "We finally have in sight the just peace we are seeking," 201–3; "What Has Happened to America?," xiv, 121–27; "When you go out to shoot rats," 83–87; White House speech on Supreme Court nominees, 210–13; White House staff speech upon resignation, lxiv–lxv, 269–76; White House statement on Kent State killings, 207–8
Nixon, Tricia (daughter), 75, 149
Nixon Doctrine, 128, 180–82
No More Vietnams (Nixon), lxvi
North Atlantic Treaty Organization (NATO), xxix, 108
North Korea, 227
North Vietnam, liv, lvi, 118–20, 170, 173–74, 176–80, 185, 190, 202, 204–5, 251
Novak, Robert, xl
nuclear warfare, 95, 135, 143, 181, 193, 250–51

O'Brien, Lawrence, lxii–lxiii
office holding, responsibilities of, 12, 65
"One China" (Nixon), 223–31
Opening Statement, Kennedy v. Nixon Debate (1960), 97–101
Orthogonian Society, xxi, 14–16
"Our best days lie ahead" (Nixon), 217–22
"Our Privileges under the Constitution" (Nixon), 7–13

Pakistan, liii, 58, 226, 228
Paris peace conference, 172, 176, 178, 179, 184, 190, 201
peace: Nixon and, lii, 248; nuclear weapons and, 95, 193; requirements for world, 194–99, 225; Soviet Union–U.S. relations and, 95–96; U.S. role in world, 154–55, 159–62, 189–90, 206, 218, 225, 238–41, 248, 250, 272; in Vietnam, lvi, 172–73, 175–80, 186, 188–90, 200–203, 205–6, 251
Pentagon, 200, 206–7
Pentagon Papers, lx
Peru, xxxi
Petersen, Henry, 266–67
Peurifoy, John, 35
Philippines, 139, 182
Picatinny Arsenal, 36
Pierce, Franklin, lxvii
"Pink Sheet" (Nixon), 60–63
"A pitiful, helpless giant" (Nixon), 203–6
Plumbers, lx–lxi
police, 126
"The Political Obituary of Richard Nixon" (television program), 105–6
"The postwar period in international relations has ended" (Nixon), 191–99
poverty, xlv, 163–69
"The present welfare system has to be judged a colossal failure" (Nixon), 163–69
presidential debates, xxxiii–xxxiv, 97–101
press: Agnew on, 209; coverage of Soviet Union in, 90; freedom of, 10, 62, 90, 106, 110; Nixon versus, 106–12, 255–58
Pressman, Lee, 23, 30
Price Waterhouse & Company, 71
Puerto Ricans, 115
"pumpkin papers," xxvi, 33

Quakerism, xix, xx, lii, 149

race: Nixon and, xxxviii, xlviii, 122; and school segregation, xxxviii, 113–16. *See also* civil rights; race riots
race riots, xiv–xv, xl, xliii, 117, 121–23, 125–27, 145–46
Reader's Digest (magazine), xiv, 121
Reagan, Ronald, xliii, lxvii
The Real War (Nixon), lxvi
Reed, Stanley F., 52
regional defense pacts, 134–36
religion, freedom of, 9. *See also* God

Remington Rand Company, 36
Republican Party: and common people, xxii; foreign policy of, xxix; Nixon and, x, xxvi, xxviii, xxxv, xxxvii–xli, 65, 114–16
Richard Nixon Library and Birthplace, xvii
Richardson, Elliot, 246–47, 250
rights: Constitutional privileges, 7–13; freedom of religion, 9; freedom of speech, 10; freedom of the press, 10, 62, 90, 106, 110; justice and, 9; Nixon on, 115, 125, 147
RN: The Memoirs of Richard Nixon (Nixon), 3–4
Rockefeller, Nelson, xliii, li, lii
Rogers, William, 177, 224
Romney, George, xlii–xliii
Roosevelt, Eleanor, 52–53
Roosevelt, Franklin D., 43–45, 47–49, 52, 155
Roosevelt, Theodore, 146, 274–75
Roosevelt and the Russians (Stettinius), 47
rule of law, 115–16, 123, 126. *See also* law and order

Sahl, Mort, xxiii
Sayre, Francis B., 53
school segregation, xxxviii, 113–16
secrecy: Bush and, lxvii; domestic policy and, xlvii; foreign policy and, l; in Nixon administration, lvii–lxiv
Securities and Exchange Commission, xlvii
segregation, xxxviii, 113–16
Seize the Moment (Nixon), lxvi
Selective Service Act (1948), 62
Silent Majority, xxii, lxviii, 146, 170, 189, 216. *See also* common people
"Silent Majority" speech (Nixon), xxii, 170–90
Simpson, O. J., xxvi
Singapore, 140
Sirica, John, 249
Six Crises (Nixon), xxvi, xxxvii, liv, 105
Smith, Dana, 66–67, 71–72
sophisticates, xxi–xxii, xxiv, xxvi, lxv, 121
South: judicial nominees from, 209–13; Nixon and electorate of the, xl, xlviii, 209
South Americans, 115
Southeast Asia, 251
Southern Christian Leadership Conference, lviii
Southern Europeans, 115

South Korea, 140, 182, 226, 227
South Vietnam, lvi, 117–20, 173–76, 179, 182–86, 201–5, 226, 227
Soviet Union: and arms treaties, 238, 250–51; China's relationship with, li, lii, 192–93; Hiss case and, 19–59; influence of, 58–59; "Kitchen Debate" and, 88–96; Nixon and, xxxii, liv; and peace, 239, 241; and Vietnam, 173, 177; world politics and, 142
space exploration, 161–62
Sparkman, John, 78
speech, freedom of, 10
"State of the World" message (Nixon), 191–99
Stein, Herb, xlix
Stettinius, Edward R., 46–48
Stevenson, Adlai: and Hiss case, 53; Nixon on, xxvii–xxviii, xxxiv, 77–78; on Nixon, xvi, xxviii
Strategic Arms Limitation Treaty, liv
Stripling, Robert, 25, 33, 44–45
Subversive Activities Control Act (1948), 61
suffrage, 11–12
Summit Conference of the Indo-Chinese Peoples, 227
surveillance, lvii–lix, lxiii, 235–36
Sweden, 58

Taiwan, 139, 223, 229–30
Tanya (Russian girl), 238, 241
technology, capitalist versus Communist, 88–96
television: "Checkers Speech" and, 64–65; Kennedy v. Nixon debate on, xxxiii–xxxiv, 97–101; in "Kitchen Debate," 89–90; 1968 campaign and, xliv; and Nixon's China visit, 223; Nixon's political fortunes and, xxxiii–xxxiv, xliv, 97–101, 105–6, 110–11, 209
Thailand, 130, 139–40, 182
"There can be no whitewash at the White House" (Nixon), 242–54
"Those bums . . . blowing up the campuses" (Nixon), 206–7
Thurmond, Strom, x, xl, xliii, xlviii
Time (magazine), xxxvi
"To lower our voices would be a simple thing" (Nixon), 153–62
travel, xiii, xxix–xxxii, liii, 88, 223–24
"Tricky Dick," xvi
Triggs, Dean, 14–15

Truman, Harry S., xxv, xxvii, 45, 99–100, 256
"two Nixons," xv–xvii, 153
Tyler, John, lxvii

unemployment, 116
United Nations: China's admission to, 108, 141; Commission for the Unification and Rehabilitation of Korea, 227; and India-Pakistan cease-fire resolution, 226, 228; Relief and Rehabilitation Administration, 62; Security Council, 226
United States, general commentary on, 89–96, 121–27, 145–49, 153–62, 189, 213–16, 221–22, 254
U.S. Bureau of Standards, 33–34, 36
U.S. Congress: and crime control legislation, 214; financial matters of members of, 67–70; Nixon in, xxi–xxvii, 19–79; presidential dealings with, xlvii, 163; and Watergate, lxiii–lxiv, 245, 259, 269
U.S. Constitution: and practical politics, ix; schoolboy essay on, 7–13; strict construction of, 210–12; Watergate and, xi
U.S. Department of Health, Education, and Welfare, lix
U.S. Justice Department, 32–35, 39, 43, 49–52, 246
U.S. State Department, l, 32–33, 35–37, 48, 223
U.S. Supreme Court, lxiv, 52, 209–13, 269–76
U.S. Treasury Department, 36

Venezuela, xxxi
Veterans' Administration, 39
videotape, 88
Vietcong, 119–20, 205
Vietnam, xxix–xxx, xxxviii, 227. *See also* North Vietnam; South Vietnam
Vietnamization, 170, 182–84, 186, 200–208
Vietnam War: 1968 election and, xli–xliii; Nixon and, xli, xliii, xlvi, liv–lvi, lviii, 7, 117–20, 124, 129–30, 134, 153, 170–90, 200–208; Pentagon Papers and, lx. *See also* antiwar sentiment
Voorhis, Jerry, xxiv

Wadleigh, Julian, 37, 41
wage and price controls, xlviii–xlix, 217
Wallace, George, xliv, lxii, 113
Walters, Vernon, 236
war. *See* military intervention; nuclear warfare

War Labor Board, 62
Washington Daily News (newspaper), 32, 50–51
Washington Post (newspaper), 31, 37, 257
Watergate scandal: blackmail and, 261–63; cover-up in, lxiii–lxiv, 232–37, 255, 259–68; meaning of, x–xi, lvii, lxvii; operations of, lxiii; rationalizations for, 7; and resignation, 269–76; tapes from, lxiv, lxvi–lxvii, 232, 234, 255, 259–69; televised address on, 242–54
"We finally have in sight the just peace we are seeking" (Nixon), 201–3
welfare, xlv, 163–69
Welles, Sumner, 35
Western Europe, 192
"What Has Happened to America?" (Nixon), xiv, 121–27
"When you go out to shoot rats" (Nixon), 83–87
White, Harry Dexter, 23, 38–39, 83
White House, Nixon's remarks on, 270–71
White House speech on Supreme Court nominees (Nixon), 210–13
White House staff speech upon resignation (Nixon), lxiv–lxv, 269
White House statement on Kent State killings (Nixon), 207–8
White House tapes, lxiv, lxvi–lxvii, 232, 234, 255, 259–69
Whittier College, xx, 14
Wilson, Woodrow, lii, 190
wiretaps, lvii, lxiii, 235–36
Witcover, Jules, xlii
Witt, Nathan, 23, 30
women, in U.S. versus Soviet Union, 91–92
Woods, Rose Mary, 260
Woodward, Bob, 233
world order, 136–37
World War II, xxii
Wyzski (judge), 53

Yalta Conference (1945), 44–45, 47–48
Yorba Linda, California, xvii–xviii, 3–4

Zabotin, Nicholi, 46